PRAISE FOR W THE ST

Weathering the Storm by Julian Roberts is an insightful and practical guide to building resilient teams and resilient individuals.

Focusing on humanistic components such as aligning personal and organisational purposes, community support, psychological safety, and diverse perspectives, this book seamlessly integrates profound insights with actionable steps, ensuring readers are both inspired and equipped to implement what they have learned. Julian's writing style is commendable for its clarity and purpose. He adeptly translates complex theories into manageable actions, making the book an essential read for anyone looking to foster resilience and strength within their teams. Whether you're an experienced leader or just starting on your leadership journey, this book offers invaluable guidance that will undoubtedly inspire and empower you. **Codie James, Founder, Coach & Transformation Consultant at Bespoke Growth Solutions**

Julian is a great storyteller who manages to unpack a broad range of crucially important topics in today's world of work in an accessible and easy-to-relate-to manner. He addresses resilience from the perspectives of purpose, belonging, and diversity while also providing tangible actions individuals and teams can take to navigate and weather the storm of the future of work. He is pragmatic, combining good research with practical real-world examples, making his recommendations tangible, easy to translate and apply to your own situation. **Dr Dieter Veldsman, Chief Scientist at AIHR**

This is a timely and practical guide for leaders at all levels, aspiring to build resilient teams capable of thriving amidst increasing uncertainty. A helpful blend of theoretical insights to foster a culture of trust and psychological safety and inspiring actionable strategies tailored to various organisational contexts.

It equips readers with the mindset, skills, and strategies needed to lead teams to become more confident and capable in an unpredictable world. **Professor Keith Jackson, Experienced Chair and Non-Executive Director**

Weathering the storm is a non-prescriptive and generous handbook for leaders looking to understand, experiment and build resilient and high-performing teams, and to create a more balanced workplace. This book is a great mix of knowledge, insights from real case studies, and practical, actionable advice as to how to create the conditions for optimal performance through team & individual resilience. A must-read in today's complex and ever-changing environment for leaders bold enough to explore their own vulnerability and growth to achieve collective resilience. **Suzie Lewis, MD & Founder, Transform for Value**

Julian Roberts' "Weathering the Storm: A Guide to Building Resilient Teams" is an invaluable resource for anyone looking to foster resilience within their team. The book's structured format, featuring an introduction, content, summary, reflection, and actionable steps for each chapter, makes it both accessible and practical. This layout encouraged me to take copious notes on how I might apply the various techniques discussed throughout the text.

Julian delves deeply into the multifaceted nature of resilience, exploring how it can be cultivated both individually and collectively. The emphasis on a diverse and inclusive approach stood out to me; it underscores the significance and importance of hearing and valuing different voices. This inclusivity fosters creativity and enables teams to "explore innovative solutions," an insight that is particularly relevant in today's dynamic work environments.

A recurring and impactful theme in the book is the importance of nurturing ourselves and each other. Julian eloquently discusses the necessity of vulnerability and the acknowledgment of mistakes as foundational elements of psychological safety. These aspects resonated deeply with me, highlighting how critical nurturing environments and vulnerability are in building trust and resilience within teams.

The practical techniques offered in the book are another

highlight. Roberts provides clear guidance on creating a sense of purpose, practicing daily gratitude, and allowing time for pause and reflection. These suggestions are presented as gentle nudges, making them easy to incorporate into daily routines. I foresee myself returning to this book frequently, using it as a reference to reinforce and refine these practices.

In summary, "Weathering the Storm" is a must-read for leaders and team members alike. Julian Roberts provides insightful, actionable strategies for building resilience, fostering creativity, and nurturing a supportive and psychologically safe team environment. This book is not just a one-time read but a lasting guide that I will continue to consult for inspiration and direction. **Dr. Lindsay Pamphilon, CEO & Principal, Orbital South Colleges**

Julian's new work is a great resource for both contemplation and practical application. His sound advice will support leaders to create healthy, not toxic, resilience in themselves and team members, by finding the sweet spot between flying too high and aiming too low.

Julian has combined shared experience, prompts for reflection, and calls to action to create exercises for use alone or with teams, all supplemented by academic corroboration and contextualised by examples from business life. The personal candour of Julian and his interviewees really adds to the depth, applicability, and authenticity of the advice.

Among the many topics covered, the book includes sections on modern hybrid / remote working practices, and on the huge benefits of workplace inclusion, making it a relevant and contemporary tool for both new leaders and all those seeking to polish their skills. **Lois Howell, Chief Executive, St Wilfred's Hospice**

Thank you Julian for this inspiring and extremely practical book to help leaders build resilience in themselves, their teams and their organisations to help us navigate through these highly uncertain times. **Susan McKee, CEO, Dental Health Services Victoria**

Join Julian as he invites you to share his learning, offering insights, encouraging reflections and giving the reader a framework for action.

This is a helpful book, written with care for the reader and an invitation to walk alongside the author in learning about team and organisational resilience. It embraces psychological safety, leading through change, the power of connection and the power of diversity and inclusion.

Drawing on personal client and broader corporate stories the need to reduce, regulate and repair to create a culture of strength and resilience is told in a compelling way. Building resilience in a remote team is addressed with care. **Dr Susan CPsychol, Business Psychologist, Author of Reinvent Yourself & Bounce Back**

The topic of resilience can be somewhat of a nebulous concept; however, Julian has successfully created a personalised, pragmatic and thought-provoking narrative on one of the most important life skills in today's modern and turbulent world. He has not only produced an absorbing read that is full of personalised and relatable examples, he has also constructed an accessible framework that can be applied across all facets of personal, team and organisational resilience.

The book brings theory and science to life with very effective and useful acronyms, analogies and stories, coupled with a reflection and action segment after each chapter which makes this book a must for the modern workplace impacting individuals, line managers, HR professionals and C-Suite Leaders. Highly commendable and I will certainly be using many of the tools and messages in the book. **Clyde Marwick, Portfolio People Director & Board Advisor**

Weathering the Storm acts as an insightful manual, offering practical steps to build strong foundations, nurture resilience, and develop fortitude. An exceptionally valuable read, rich with actionable steps, examples and advice. Julian's approach makes this book a timeless resource for leaders and teams alike, my only hope is that leaders read it before they need it. **Elsa Hogan, Vice President Rolls-Royce Defence**

This book teaches us how to build individual and team resilience through Julian's extensive research of established theories, and case studies from his broad and diverse professional and personal experiences – from coaching CEOs to leading an international yoghurt commercial team.

I particularly like how Julian has used crisis scenarios, understood through different perspectives and applied the learnings in peacetime conditions. I feel this approach will support sustainable resilience and continuous growth. I also like the inclusion of therapeutic perspectives and practices, like mindfulness. Whilst these might still be relatively new concepts in some corporate settings, the book contains a set of actions at the end of each chapter, making it straightforward for anyone to apply within their setting.

This isn't a book that I'll read once. I look forward to it serving as a reference guide and toolkit for me to use independently and with my team. **Cady Phipps, People & Change Expert**

WEATHERING THE STORM

A GUIDE TO BUILDING RESILIENT TEAMS

JULIAN ROBERTS

COPYRIGHT JULIAN ROBERTS 2024

TABLE OF CONTENTS

ABOUT THE AUTHOR XI

FOREWORD XIII

ACKNOWLEDGEMENTS XV

INTRODUCTION : THE WHY 1

PART ONE
ESTABLISHING A RESILIENT FOUNDATION

CHAPTER ONE:
CREATING TEAM/ORGANISATIONAL PURPOSE 17

CHAPTER TWO:
CREATING RESILIENT PROCESSES 33

PART TWO
NURTURING INDIVIDUAL AND TEAM RESILIENCE

CHAPTER THREE:
CREATING PERSONAL RESILIENCE 57

CHAPTER FOUR:
CREATING PSYCHOLOGICAL SAFETY 79

PART THREE
DEVELOPING RESILIENT LEADERSHIP

CHAPTER FIVE:
CREATING RESILIENT LEADERSHIP 101

CHAPTER SIX:
CREATING DIVERSITY AND INCLUSION 125

PART FOUR
EMBRACING ADAPTABILITY IN THE FUTURE OF WORK

CHAPTER SEVEN:
CREATING HYBRID/REMOTE RESILIENT TEAMS 147

AND FINALLY... 169

ABOUT THE AUTHOR

Julian Roberts is an experienced executive coach, organisational consultant, and author specialising in building resilient teams and leaders. With a solid background in corporate leadership roles and a master's degree in Psychology, Julian brings a unique blend of practical experience and academic knowledge to his work. He combines evidence-based psychological principles with real-world strategies to help organisations not just survive, but thrive in volatile, uncertain, complex, and ambiguous (VUCA) environments. His approach focuses on developing both individual and team resilience, recognising that these elements are crucial for organisational success in today's rapidly changing business landscape.

When not helping organisations navigate turbulent times, Julian practices what he preaches by embracing his own resilience through cold water swimming, a practice known for its mental and physical health benefits. He also enjoys spending time outdoors with his family, trail running, and continuously expanding his perspectives through reading and engaging with diverse viewpoints. This commitment to personal growth and resilience informs and enhances his professional work, allowing him to bring fresh insights and authentic experiences to his clients and readers.

Connect with Julian

Website: https://www.julianrobertsconsulting.com/

LinkedIn: https://www.linkedin.com/in/julesroberts/

Email: julian@julianrobertsconsulting.com

FOREWORD

In today's dynamic and often unpredictable world, the ability of a team to adapt and thrive amidst adversity is paramount. Change is a constant. It's the new norm. The challenges we face—ranging from global market fluctuations to global supply chain disruption require teams that are not only robust but also resilient. "Weathering the Storm: A Guide to Building Resilient Teams" serves as an essential operating manual for leaders and our wider communities alike, offering insights and strategies to navigate these turbulent times effectively.

This book is a testament to the power of collective strength and the indomitable spirit of teamwork. It goes beyond merely providing advice; it offers a comprehensive framework for cultivating resilience within teams. Drawing from real-world examples, expert analyses, and practical strategies, Julian illuminates the path to building teams that can withstand pressure and emerge stronger.

As someone who has led teams through both calm and stormy periods, I understand first-hand the critical role resilience plays. Changing mindsets, culture and organisational effectiveness is tough for all leaders. Getting knock backs, finding the power to recover and keep moving forward requires a deeper set of skills. It's about more than just surviving challenges; it's about growing and evolving through them. This guide explores the core principles of resilient teams, emphasising the importance of trust, communication, and a shared sense of purpose. It shows how these elements, along with fostering a purpose-led culture, can transform obstacles into opportunities for growth and galvanise teams and organisations to release their super strength.

"Weathering the Storm" equips you with the tools to foster a culture of support, adaptability, and innovation. A purpose-led culture not only unites team members but also drives their efforts towards meaningful and collective goals. As you delve into its pages, you will gain the knowledge and confidence to lead your team through any storm, ensuring not only survival but also success.

Prepare to embark on a journey towards resilience and enduring achievement. Welcome to "Weathering the Storm: A Guide to Building Resilient Teams."

Mike England

CEO Flowtech Plc

ACKNOWLEDGEMENTS

Firstly, I would like to say a big thank you to my wife, Lin, who has always supported me in everything I do, whether that is to leave the corporate world and start a coaching practice, or to study for my Psychology Masters, and now this book. Not only encouraging, she is also challenging and keeps me very grounded in what I do.

Secondly, my daughter, Abbie, who was part of the editing process, and treated me with such objectivity ensuring I produced a readable book.

To the several leaders who kindly offered their time and support whilst I interviewed them, and have been included in this book: Allegra Chapman, Dipak Duggal, Jim Hotaling, Jona Wright, Julie Kapsalis, Mike England, Paul Randall, Richard Searle, Suzie Lewis, and Tracy Aust.

To those who I have interviewed on my podcast – Helping Organisations Thrive, whose wisdom has been included in the book: Allegra Chapman, Chico Chakravorty, Jonathan Fields and Tarin Calmeyer.

And to the All Systems Row team (Andrea Harwood, Charlie Cooper, Jess Plail, Lia Evans and Steph Toogood), who I had the privilege of coaching for 12 months in preparation for their GB Row challenge around Great Britain, whose insights, learnings and experiences are shared throughout the book. And also to Mark Upton, CEO of MyVision Oxfordshire, for not only allowing their coaching experience to be used as a case study in the book, but for their openness and courage to embrace the principles in this book.

And to those who pre-read the book and provided invaluable feedback, thank you for your generosity of time and support: Cady Allen, Clyde Marwick, Codies James, Dieter Veldsman, Elsa Hogan, Professor Keith Jackson, Lindsay Pamphilon, Lois Howell, Mike England, Dr Susan Kahn, Susan McKee and Suzie Lewis.

And finally to all of my clients, with whom I not only have the privilege of seeing transformation, but also have the opportunity to learn and hone my craft.

INTRODUCTION : THE WHY

The Why behind Weathering the Storm: A Guide to Building Resilient Teams

As a leader, you have three guarantees:

The first is uncertainty. Despite my efforts, I know it is impossible to predict the future. Nobody could have predicted what transpired with the recent war in Ukraine and how it would affect the global economy. Nobody was able to predict the pandemic. Life is unpredictable and, as a leader, you will always face uncertainty. Next, I can guarantee that you will experience failure, especially if you are pushing the boundaries of yourself and your team to innovate and create new ways of working. Failure can be beneficial if the lessons learned by it lead to growth. And the final guarantee: change itself. It's a concept so frequently discussed that it has become almost cliché to say, "Change is here to stay." Yet, despite its overuse, this statement holds true. The constancy of change is an undeniable reality in our world.

In the face of uncertainty, failure, and change, how do we navigate and lead ourselves and our teams? A unique perspective comes from my experience coaching a team of five female rowers attempting to circumnavigate Great Britain in the summer of 2022. A 2,000-mile journey that would put them in the record books. In addition to battling the exhaustion that comes with 24 hours of rowing each day, they would have to contend with changing tides, variable weather, and navigating shipping lanes. It was a formidable challenge. In June 2022, they left Tower Bridge in London, travelled down the River Thames to the sea, turned south, and circumnavigated Great Britain in a clockwise direction. Everything was going smoothly until they came off the coast of Wales, approximately 500 miles into their journey, having already endured rain, storms, exhaustion, and a variety of other obstacles. At this point, they were heading to the southeast of Ireland to anchor, having received news of a particularly severe storm approaching. The storm was expected to arrive within 18 to 24 hours, so they believed they would make it at their current pace.

However, the weather does not always behave as predicted, and the storm arrived eight hours earlier than expected. As a result, the team was caught in the storm, which was generating 20 to 30-foot waves and unfortunately damaged a few of their boat's components, rendering them unable to steer and control the boat effectively. Now with limited control, they were being dragged towards one of the busiest shipping lanes in the UK. This caused them to initiate a planned rescue with the RNLI, who then came and rescued them and brought them back to safety. The lifeboat crew reflected that "this was the worst storm they had experienced since 1972". This team, despite their failure, was incredibly resilient; they desired to get back out onto the water the moment they got to the coast of Wales, which I believed was sheer madness. However, because they had lost expensive key equipment due to the storm, they were unfortunately unable to return to the sea. Regardless of this disappointing news, they got back up, drew lessons from the experience, and were eager to take on additional challenges in their lives. This is what I consider the epitome of a resilient team: a team that can navigate uncertainty, deal with failure, and effectively adapt to change. You may not be in a boat in a storm, but you will still have to face the storms within your team and organisation.

Globally, organisations are confronted with a plethora of complexities, obstacles, and shifting environments, which creates uncertainties that may affect their existence. During the pandemic, the capability of organisations and employees to respond positively to the challenges of the pandemic crisis became critically important - not just navigating the crisis but creating a place to thrive and be sustainable and competitive for the future. Significant attention was focused on developing resilience for the individual, with less attention on the organisation and teams. We are facing uncertainty on a level that we have not seen in our lifetime, and according to the World Economic Outlook Report, October 2022, "Global economic activity is experiencing a broad-based and sharper-than-expected slowdown, with inflation higher than seen in several decades. The cost-of-living crisis, tightening financial conditions in most regions, Russia's invasion of Ukraine, and the lingering COVID-19 pandemic all weigh heavily on the outlook." We are aware that the world we live in is VUCA, which stands for volatility, uncertainty, complexity, and ambiguity. Volatility means that change happens quickly and in ways that are hard to predict. Uncertainty means that neither the present nor the future is clear. Complexity: Many factors interact with each other and can lead to chaos and misunderstanding. Ambiguity means that things are not clear or that people are not aware of what is going on.

So, how do we navigate such challenges within our teams? We can often fall into the trap, that gathering a group of individually resilient people will automatically create a resilient team. On the contrary, even highly resilient people can suffer from issues of communication, leadership conflicts, accountability challenges and different mental models in how they operate together. However, it is worth noting that some studies have shown that resilient employees are not only better equipped to deal with challenges but also to navigate and overcome these events more successfully, and to see the positive meaning around negative experiences - this enables them to be more flexible, and agile and perform better over time (Tugade & Fredrickson, 2004; Youssef & Luthans, 2007).

According to the American Psychological Association, resilience is "the process of adapting well in the face of adversity, trauma, tragedy, threats, or significant sources of stress." I would add that it is also about being able to grow stronger through challenges and not just survive, but be the individual and team that grows. The human ability to confront, overcome, and even grow from adversity is known as resilience. Being resilient means having the mindset that everything is possible. It is the capacity to set and reassess personal goals as you go from days to weeks to months to years to attain your target. Sometimes it involves leveraging hardship to discover the doors that lead to our actual purpose in life. One of the biggest lessons I learned is that we don't have a fixed amount of resilience. It's like a muscle - we can build it up. This book is all about helping you with tools, pragmatic theories, and experiences to build this resilience into your teams, strengthening the "muscle" of resilience.

When considering teams within organisations, it would be beneficial to understand how teams interplay with the concept of resilience. Teams in the workplace can be defined as "interdependent groups of individuals who share responsibility for particular organisational outcomes." (Sundstrom et al., 1990). Since teams take a central role in the modern workplace, and with the inevitability of adversities, there has been an increased interest in finding the various ways teams can navigate through such crises (Mathieu, Tannenbaum, Donsbach & Alliger, 2014). A recent study (Traylor et al., 2020) found that one of the best ways for teams to be equipped for a crisis is by consciously boosting team resilience.

Organisational and team resilience have two different perspectives. The first is simply the ability to bounce back from challenges, difficulties and adversity (Sutcliffe & Vogus, 2003). The other perspective is where the team or organisation gains the skill of developing new capabilities and expanding the organisation's ability to foster new ideas and thinking. In essence, this perspective is all about creating learning to enable the organisation to thrive into the future, going beyond just bouncing back (Lengnick-Hall & Beck Legninck, 2011). It was cited by Bennett et al. (2010) that "resilience is an individual trait that can be seen as a social factor that exists in teams." This is consistent with Bandura's efficacy theory concept (1997), which states that "a group has shared beliefs in its capabilities to establish and deliver the course of action to enable the group to succeed." According to Blatt (2009), resilience is essential for teams and organisations to succeed. The way teams respond to the changes in their environment depends on a variety of complex bottom-up experiences that develop over time from individual behaviour, interactions, mental models, and cognition among team members (Kozlowski & Klein, 2000). The definition of team resilience proposed by Morgan et al. (2013) is widely accepted in the literature; they defined team resilience as a dynamic, psychosocial process that protects a group of individuals from the potential negative impact of stressors they collectively encounter. It consists of the processes by which team members use their individual and collective resources to adapt positively to adversity.

In addition to the obvious benefits of a resilient team, such as greater adaptability to change and the ability to handle stress and challenges, there are other benefits to building resilient teams. These include increased productivity and performance, better problem-solving and decision-making, improved communication and collaboration, increased job satisfaction and engagement, and a higher retention rate. In the fast-paced landscape of the modern workplace, where change is constant and uncertainty is a given, team resilience has emerged as a beacon guiding organisations through turbulent waters. The ability of teams not just to endure challenges but to thrive in the face of adversity is a testament to their resilience. This book is an exploration of the multifaceted journey toward building and sustaining resilience within teams.

Toxic resilience

Before going any further with the book, it is important to address the concept of toxic resilience—an unhealthy approach to coping with stress and challenges that can significantly impact an individual's mental, emotional, and physical well-being. While resilience is seen as a positive thing, involving the ability to overcome adversity, toxic resilience can take a harmful turn. This detrimental mindset manifests in various ways, such as overworking leading to burnout, suppressing emotions to appear strong, avoiding seeking help due to perceived weakness, setting unrealistic standards resulting in chronic stress, struggling with boundaries between work and personal life, stigmatising vulnerability, impaired relationships, and contributing to physical health issues through chronic stress.

I was discussing this with Suzie Lewis, MD for Transform for Value, and she came up with a great analogy between "rubber band resilience" (bouncing back at any cost) and "creative resilience". She dislikes the former, likening it to pushing through difficulties without considering the long-term consequences. Suzie shared that when she completed her first marathon, her knees gave in, but she still carried on until the end because she was determined to finish. Suzie dealt with the physical consequences of this decision up to two weeks later. And now, years later, she has an issue with her back. However, "creative resilience", akin to water finding a way, involves adaptability, an abundance of thinking, and a proactive approach to challenges.

Another leader I spoke to about this also shared a similar view on ensuring we don't fall into the trap of toxic resilience: Dipak Duggal, Director of Medical Affairs for BD, shares a personal story that may resonate with you. Drawing from the lived experience of his daughter Phoebe Duncan-Duggal, Dipak says "It's akin to the scenario of kids participating in the Duke of Edinburgh's Award, where a team of individuals faces challenges. As parents we've listened to the stories of when after a gruelling hike in the rain, these youngsters find themselves in tears, struggling to set up wet tents in the Lake District. The truth is that not everyone responds the same way. Some individuals excel at rallying their spirits, embracing challenges with a 'what's next' attitude. However, it's vital to recognise that not everyone possesses this sort of resilience. It's perfectly acceptable for someone to acknowledge when they're not coping. Establishing channels for expressing vulnerability, whether through a stress hotline or a simple admission of struggle, can serve as a valuable indicator that the team might be facing collective challenges. By creating an environment where individuals feel comfortable admitting when something feels undoable, we open the door to collective problem-solving and shared resilience."

To prevent toxic resilience, it's essential to foster a culture that encourages a healthy work-life balance: open communication about mental health, destigmatisation of vulnerability, and proactive support systems to ensure individuals feel empowered to seek help without fear of judgment. Leaders play a pivotal role in setting the tone for such a culture, emphasising the importance of well-being, acknowledging the realities of challenges, and promoting a collaborative approach to problem-solving. Role modelling by leaders becomes particularly crucial in this context—leaders who openly share their challenges, embrace vulnerability and prioritise self-care set a powerful example. By showcasing that seeking help and prioritising mental health are signs of strength rather than weakness, leaders create an environment where employees feel supported and encouraged to adopt healthy coping mechanisms. Additionally, providing resources for stress management, offering flexibility in work arrangements, and encouraging regular breaks contribute to a supportive environment where individuals can thrive without succumbing to the detrimental effects of toxic resilience.

Why team resilience matters

Team resilience is a key factor in the success of any business going beyond the simple framework of crisis management. For organisations aspiring not only to weather storms but to thrive in the dynamic landscape of the modern business world, developing team resilience is a strategic imperative. Resilient teams operate as catalysts for organisational agility, innovation, and sustained high performance. The impact of resilient teams extends beyond crisis response; it becomes ingrained in the organisational culture, steering it toward continuous improvement. Rather than viewing challenges as insurmountable roadblocks, resilient teams perceive them as stepping stones toward excellence. This mindset shift permeates the entire organisation, creating a dynamic environment where adaptability and a solution-oriented approach thrive.

Team resilience is intricately linked with individual well-being, especially in an era marked by the prevalence of burnout and stress. Beyond the collective ability to navigate challenges, resilient teams prioritise the health and happiness of their members. This dual focus becomes a defining factor in organisational success, as the well-being of individuals contributes significantly to overall team performance. In cultivating resilience, teams create a profound sense of belonging, purpose, and fulfilment among their members. This goes beyond the usual idea of professional success; it involves making the workplace a place where people can grow professionally and individually. Resilient teams, by promoting a supportive and nurturing environment, not only weather storms but also become the bedrock for individual growth and organisational prosperity in the long run.

The structure of this book

The approach of each chapter follows a structured format of "Insight, Reflection, Action." This format is designed to provide a comprehensive and actionable guide for individuals, team leaders, and organisational decision-makers. Let's break down the significance of each component:

Insight

Purpose: The "Insight" section introduces the key concept or theme of the chapter. It provides deep insights into the importance, principles, and dynamics of the specific aspect of team resilience being explored. This section aims to offer a foundational understanding of the topic, laying the groundwork for the practical application that follows.

Reflection

Understanding and internalisation: The "Reflection" section serves as a bridge between theoretical understanding and personal application. It prompts you to reflect on your own experiences, challenges, and the current state of your teams. Through guided questions and prompts, you are encouraged to connect the theoretical insights with their real-world context, which helps you get a deeper comprehension of how the ideas relate to your circumstances.

Action

Practical application: The "Action" section translates insights into tangible, practical steps, providing you with strategies to implement within your teams. These actions are designed to be realistic and adaptable to various team environments. The goal is to empower you to take immediate steps toward building and sustaining resilience within your teams.

This structured format aims to go beyond theoretical discussions by providing you with tools and strategies you can actively apply. It acknowledges that true learning and transformation occur when insights are internalised and translated into actionable steps within the unique context of each team and organisation. This is not a theoretical exploration of abstract concepts. It is a pragmatic guide, a roadmap for individuals, team leaders, and organisational decision-makers seeking to cultivate and sustain resilience within their teams.

I have developed four main principles. The journey begins with an exploration of the foundation – the role of purpose-driven organisations in shaping resilient teams. Principle 1: Establishing a resilient foundation explores the profound impact of a clear and compelling organisational purpose on team dynamics, decision-making, and culture. Chapter 1 focuses on creating team/organisational purpose, while chapter 2 explores the importance of creating resilient processes. The insights gained from understanding the essence of purpose set the stage for the subsequent chapters, where we explore the multifaceted aspects of team resilience.

Principle 2: Nurturing individual and team resilience builds upon the foundation established in Part 1. In Chapter 3, personal resilience is discussed, emphasising the role that each member's wellbeing plays in building resilient teams. To allow team members to flourish and give their greatest contributions, Chapter 4 explores the vital function that psychological safety plays.

Principle 3: Developing resilient leadership shifts the focus to the crucial role of leadership in building resilient teams. Chapter 5 explores the strategies and mindset required for creating resilient leadership, while chapter 6 emphasises the importance of creating diversity and inclusion within teams, harnessing the strength of diverse perspectives and experiences.

Principle 4: Embracing adaptability in the future of work looks ahead, addressing the challenges and opportunities presented by the evolving landscape of work. Chapter 7 provides insights and strategies for creating hybrid/remote resilient teams, equipping leaders with the tools to navigate the complexities of distributed workforces.

From creating a psychologically safe environment to learning from failures, from role modelling resilience to fostering collaborative strategies – the book navigates the diverse terrain of team resilience. By exploring these critical aspects, leaders and teams can develop the skills, mindset, and practices necessary to thrive in the face of challenges and uncertainty.

Who Can Benefit from This Book?

This is a comprehensive guide tailored to meet the diverse needs of its readership. It caters to a broad audience, ensuring its relevance for various roles within an organisation. Whether you find yourself as an individual team member aspiring to fortify your resilience; a team leader eager to cultivate a culture of resilience; or a decision-maker at the organisational level striving to optimise overall team performance, this book offers practical strategies applicable at every tier. For team members seeking personal growth and enhanced resilience, this book provides insights and tools that empower individuals to navigate challenges effectively. The book offers actionable advice, encouraging self-reflection and the development of skills that contribute to personal and professional well-being.

Team leaders will discover a wealth of practical strategies to inspire and empower their teams. The book explores leadership principles that enhance resilience, creating an environment where team members can thrive, collaborate, and overcome obstacles. It serves as a valuable resource for those aiming to elevate their leadership skills and enhance the resilience of their teams.

Human resources professionals can leverage the content of this book to design and implement programs that enhance team well-being and performance. The book addresses key aspects of team dynamics and individual well-being, offering insights that can be incorporated into HR strategies to create a workplace culture that supports the holistic growth of employees.

Executives and decision-makers gain valuable perspectives on the broader impact of fostering team resilience on organisational success. The book connects the dots between team dynamics, resilience, and overall performance, providing a strategic understanding of how investing in team resilience contributes to long-term organisational prosperity. It offers a roadmap for decision-makers to align their organisational goals with the cultivation of resilient teams, positioning the company for sustained success in today's dynamic business landscape.

A Call to Action: Navigating Challenges Together

I invite you to not only read but to actively engage with the material. Team resilience is not a theoretical concept to be discussed in boardrooms; it is a lived experience, shaped by the actions and attitudes of every team member. The insights provided are not static principles but dynamic tools to be wielded in the ever-evolving landscape of work. Consider this book as your companion on the path toward creating teams that not only survive challenges but thrive amid uncertainty. Each chapter is an opportunity for exploration, introspection, and transformation. The goal is not just to disseminate knowledge but to empower you to take meaningful actions that propel your teams toward resilience and success.

Behind the pages: A journey into team resilience

In the exploration of team resilience, it is only fitting to share the behind-the-scenes journey that led to the creation of this book. This section offers a glimpse into my personal experiences as a leader, a coach, and an interviewer, providing a context for the insights and strategies presented throughout the book.

My leadership journey

As a leader, I have navigated the ever-changing landscape of organisational dynamics, experiencing both the triumphs and tribulations that shape one's leadership philosophy. Throughout my career, I have witnessed firsthand the profound impact that resilience has on a team's ability to weather storms and emerge stronger on the other side. Whether it was navigating disappointing results of launching new products into Tesco as a sales leader or managing the difficulties of a company's manufacturing site employees who were on strike for three weeks, thus impacting the supply of our products into the marketplace, each experience has taught me valuable lessons about the importance of adaptability, perseverance, and resilience in the face of setbacks.

Through these experiences, I have come to understand that

resilience is not just about bouncing back from adversity; it is about the capacity to learn, grow, and adapt in the face of challenges. It is about developing a mindset that sees setbacks as opportunities for growth and innovation. As a leader, my role is to create an environment that nurtures this resilience, providing the support, resources, and guidance that enables my team to thrive in the face of uncertainty. Looking back on my leadership journey, I am grateful for the lessons learned and the insights gained. Each victory and setback has contributed to my understanding of what it takes to build and lead resilient teams, and I remain committed to building resilience within my teams, knowing that it is the key to unlocking our full potential and achieving sustained success.

Coaching teams toward resilience

In my role as a coach, I've had the privilege of working closely with diverse teams facing unique challenges. The coaching journey has been an immersive experience, allowing me to witness firsthand the transformative power of resilience. Through one-on-one sessions and team workshops, I've seen individuals and teams not just bounce back from adversity but emerge stronger and more cohesive. My coaching engagements have been varied and tailored to the specific needs of each team. In some instances, I've worked with clients to scenario plan for the future, helping them anticipate potential challenges and develop strategies to navigate them effectively. These sessions have focused on cultivating a proactive mindset, enhancing adaptability, and building the skills necessary to respond to change with resilience.

In other cases, I've embarked on more comprehensive, long-term engagements, such as a six-month programme dedicated to developing resilience within a team. These experiences have given me a deep understanding of team dynamics, enabling me to identify areas for growth, and implement targeted interventions to strengthen their resilience. By focusing on key aspects such as improving psychological safety, enhancing communication, and building trust, these engagements have resulted in teams that are better equipped to handle adversity and thrive in the face of challenges. Regardless of the specific approach or duration of the coaching engagement, the overarching goal remains the same: to build resilient teams. This coaching journey has provided me with valuable insights into constructing resilient teams.

Interviews with resilient leaders

Engaging in discussions with leaders from diverse industries has given me some valuable perspectives. Through numerous interviews, I've had the privilege of exploring the journeys of individuals who have effectively nurtured resilience within their teams. These leaders openly shared their tales of victories, challenges, and the methodologies they used to instil resilience in the midst of uncertainty. You'll discover insights derived from these interviews offering essential perspectives. One particularly enlightening platform for these conversations has been my podcast, "Helping Organisations Thrive." This podcast has served as a space for candid and thought-provoking discussions with leaders who have navigated the complexities of building resilient teams in various contexts. From executives in multinational corporations to entrepreneurs in startups to world record holders; each guest has brought a unique lens to the topic of resilience. Through our dialogues, we've explored the practical strategies, mindset shifts, and leadership approaches that have proven effective in increasing resilience at both the individual and organisational levels. These insights have provided listeners with valuable lessons they can apply in their leadership journeys.

Interviewing resilient leaders has been a transformative experience, as it has highlighted the commonalities and differences in how resilience manifests across industries and leadership styles. Despite the diversity of their backgrounds and experiences, these leaders have consistently emphasised the importance of creating a culture of trust, empowering their teams to learn from failures, and leading with empathy and adaptability. Their stories serve as powerful reminders that resilience is not just a theoretical concept but a practical necessity for thriving in today's ever-changing business landscape. By integrating their insights throughout this book and sharing them through the "Helping Organisations Thrive" podcast, I aim to inspire and equip readers and listeners with the wisdom and strategies gleaned from these exceptional leaders, ultimately empowering them to cultivate resilience within their teams and organisations.

Bringing theory to life

This book is a narrative of my experiences and a bridge between theory and practice. It is an acknowledgement that the insights presented here are not abstract concepts but lessons learned from years of experience in coaching and leading teams. It is a testament to the real-world application of the principles of team resilience.

In the spirit of navigating challenges together, let us embark on this journey of learning, growing, and thriving as resilient teams.

PART ONE
ESTABLISHING A RESILIENT FOUNDATION

CHAPTER ONE:
CREATING TEAM/ ORGANISATIONAL PURPOSE

What you will gain from this chapter

A deeper understanding of the significance of purpose in driving team resilience and organisational success.

Insights into what defines a purpose-driven organisation and real-world examples of companies that have successfully integrated purpose into their strategies.

Knowledge of how purpose contributes to intrinsic motivation, team cohesion, and adaptability in the face of challenges.

A practical, step-by-step approach to crafting a compelling team purpose statement that aligns with the broader organisational mission.

Strategies for effective communication, strategic alignment, and fostering a sense of ownership among employees in the pursuit of a purpose-driven culture.

An appreciation for the importance of encouraging employees to explore and align their purposes with the organisation's purpose, leading to heightened engagement and a stronger connection between individuals and the collective mission.

Insight: Your team's why

The concept of purpose has gained popularity both in business and personal spheres. After getting her master's degree my daughter was discussing her career goals with me. She realised how important it was to have a clear sense of purpose when making long-term decisions. While I recognised the value of understanding one's purpose, I have always stressed the beauty of not feeling confined to having all the answers before taking action. Life, much like a captivating story, has a way of unveiling facets of our purpose as we navigate its twists and turns. Reflecting on my story, I came to an understanding of my own purpose after leaving the business world; a statement that changed the focus of my career was "unlocking human potential." This purpose became clear to me as I retraced the steps of my two-decade career in sales. Although crafting sales strategies and spearheading initiatives brought a sense of accomplishment, it was the human connection that was a part of my job that really resonated with me. It made me happy to understand what made each person unique, to identify their latent talents, and to nurture their growth. And so, the phrase "unlocking human potential" etched itself as the cornerstone of my purpose.

As the crossroads of my post-corporate journey approached, the idea of becoming a coach emerged, blatantly clear that it fits with my purpose. The unique responsibility of a coach, which involves helping people reach their full potential, pushed me to undertake new training. What started as a quest to help people reach their full potential grew into a bigger mission: to help leaders and teams become more resilient. This newfound interest, which I discovered while working with clients, helped me write this book. Each page is a testament to the evolution of my purpose - developing from unlocking individual potential to cultivating resilience within teams and leaders.

While discussions about purpose-led organisations abound, especially in attracting millennial and Gen Z talent, it is noteworthy that a sense of purpose also contributes to employee engagement and retention. These positive aspects enhance both individual and organisational value. I believe that the primary reason for an organisation to adopt a purpose-driven approach is to cultivate resilience, enabling not just survival but thriving and ensuring sustainability. Julie Kapsalis, CEO and Principal at North East Surrey College of Technology (NESCOT) emphasises the importance of a shared sense of purpose. She questions whether the motivation for hard work stems from external factors like achieving a certain accreditation or from a genuine belief in the fundamental mission of providing the best education and destinations for her students. Julie sees a shared purpose within her leadership team as a powerful motivator for going the extra mile and achieving their goals. Their ambition to move from a "good" to an "outstanding" rating in the next Ofsted inspection is not driven by trying to 'peak' for the inspection but by a deep commitment to ensuring every student receives the best education and opportunities every single day. In exploring purpose-driven organisations, it becomes crucial to understand what defines them, how their purpose manifests, and why it contributes to resilience. Equally important is the exploration of how to create a purpose-driven culture. These are the questions I explore within this chapter.

What is a purpose-driven organisation?

While the significance of purpose-led companies is widely acknowledged in today's business landscape, a universally accepted definition remains elusive. Various authors diverge in their emphasis, with one group focusing on a company's product and brand values, echoing Accenture's view that function is "the reason for something's existence." Another perspective centres on the broader environmental and social impact of a company, aligning closely with environmental, social, and governance (ESG) concepts. A compelling definition proposed by Henderson and van den Steen (2015) defines a company's purpose as "a concrete goal or objective that goes beyond maximising profits." This goes further than specific activities like donations or sponsorships, encapsulating the core "raison d'être" of a company, guiding all of its activities and acting as its core philosophy.

Illustratively, TOMS, a shoe and eyewear company, integrates its purpose, "we believe in a more equitable world," by giving a third of its profits for grassroots good. Their strategy aligns with their purpose through the use of sustainable materials, ethical sourcing, fair labour practices, and employee participation in social impact initiatives. Regular impact reporting underscores their commitment to transparency. Similarly, Microsoft, with its purpose to "empower every person and every organisation on the planet to achieve more," successfully navigated the pandemic by facilitating remote work and online education. Their focus on employee well-being and mental health showcased a purpose-driven approach that guided strategic decisions and adaptation to changing circumstances. This commitment to social responsibility contributed to increased revenue and stock value. And finally, Moderna, a biotechnology company, thrived during the pandemic due to its purpose-driven mission to deliver impact through mRNA medicines. The rapid development of a highly efficacious COVID-19 vaccine showcased their commitment to innovation and science. A purpose-driven culture fostered collaboration, risk-taking, and resilience - crucial attributes during unprecedented challenges. Moderna's unwavering commitment to societal impact positioned it as a thriving entity during the pandemic and beyond. Table 1 further displays some other examples of company purpose statements.

Table 1: Purpose statements of companies

Company	Purpose Statement
Unilever	To make sustainable living commonplace
GlaxoSmithKline	Do more, feel better, live longer
Rolls-Royce	To pioneer the power that matters
Vodafone	Connecting for a better future
Tesco	To create value for customers to earn their lifetime loyalty
Disney	To entertain, inform and inspire people around the globe through the power of unparalleled storytelling
Patagonia	We're in business to save our home planet
Airbus	We pioneer sustainable aerospace for a safe and united world
Philips	To improve people's health and well-being through meaningful innovation

Having a sense of purpose in your business goes beyond mere numerical metrics, sales figures, and profits. Mike England, CEO of Flowtech Plc, reflects on his personal experience at RS Group plc, underscoring the crucial role of a shared purpose in cultivating resilience at both individual and organisational levels. According to Mike, there exists a meaningful connection between individual resilience, team resilience, and business resilience, with a sense of purpose being integral to each. He emphasises that ever since he discovered his purpose, a compelling and motivating force, he has actively encouraged his teams to uncover their purposes too. Mike contends that awareness of purpose and alignment with the company's broader mission are essential for engaging teams and equipping them to navigate challenges and overcome setbacks.

Consider the rowing team that I coached, embarking on the ambitious journey to circumnavigate Great Britain, a formidable 2,000 mile journey, with the aspiration of setting a world record. Although the team encountered unforeseen challenges, requiring a rescue operation only 500 miles into the endeavour, their journey held a more profound purpose than the mere pursuit of a record. In essence, the rowing team was a contributor to a greater cause by providing valuable climate change data for a University of Portsmouth study. This shift from their original sporting goal underscores the importance of fostering a purpose that goes beyond specific key performance indicators (KPIs) or narrowly defined objectives, ultimately broadening individuals' perspectives. While the team may have fallen short of completing the circumnavigation, the first 500 miles of their trip were very important to the broader story of climate change research. This parallel focus underscores the resilience and adaptability required in the face of unforeseen challenges, ultimately allowing the team to make a tangible and meaningful impact where it was least expected. Despite the setback, their addition to climate change data shows the power of purpose-driven efforts, showing that even when things seem to fail, success can be found when aligned with a purpose that goes beyond set goals.

Tesla, renowned for electric cars and Elon Musk, epitomises a purpose-driven approach. While many associate Tesla with being the leading provider of electric cars, their mission, "accelerating the world's transition to sustainable energy," surpasses the scope of vehicle manufacturing. Regardless of one's role at Tesla, whether in manufacturing, sales, or finance, employees contribute to a global cause, actively participating in an initiative to expedite the world's adoption of renewable energy. In a thorough examination of the extended performance of companies driven by purpose compared to those primarily fixated on sales and profits, the book 'Firms of Endearment' conducted a study spanning a decade (2002 to 2012). The findings showed that companies propelled by purpose, stakeholder orientation, and a robust caring culture, consistently outperformed their counterparts driven solely by sales and profits. Purpose-driven companies achieved an impressive annual average return on equity of 13.1%, significantly outpacing the 4.12% return of companies focused primarily on sales and profits. This stark contrast in performance underscores the tangible financial benefits of adopting a purpose-led approach to business. Essentially, integrating a purpose into business operations proves to be a catalyst for success, influencing performance on multiple levels and ultimately contributing to sustained profitability.

How does this connect to cultivating team resilience?

In March 2020, the UK government's announcement about the onset of the coronavirus pandemic and the subsequent lockdown plunged us into a realm of unknowns. It was a global shockwave, leaving individuals and organisations grappling with a chaotic state of not knowing what lay ahead. There was no playbook, no roadmap for individuals or leaders to follow. With all of this uncertainty, I found myself consulting with CEOs, some of whom were clients, who were battling with the profound impacts of the unfolding events.

One such CEO reached out to me, seeking advice on how to navigate the pandemic. It was during this that a fundamental question emerged: "What is the purpose of your business?" This CEO led a purpose-driven organisation, and as he reiterated the company's purpose, it sparked the question: "Has the pandemic altered your purpose in any way?" His response was "Not really." I said, "Okay, while the fundamental purpose remains unchanged, the 'how' and the 'timing' might have shifted in how you are going to achieve it." It became apparent that revisiting the team, reinforcing the purpose, and using it as a source of energy to generate ideas were essential steps to steer through the challenges posed by the pandemic. Thinking about this advice, the CEO led his team in a useful exercise. By revisiting their purpose, they breathed new life into their collective enthusiasm. Energised by the shared sense of purpose, the team embarked on a collaborative journey to devise strategies that would not only address the uncertainties brought about by the pandemic but also keep them aligned with their overarching mission.

This narrative vividly illustrates the transformative power of a well-defined purpose in guiding a team through the challenges within their organisation. By taking a step back and gaining perspective from the broader picture outlined by their purpose, the team found themselves better equipped to address and navigate complexities effectively. It showcases the resilience and adaptability that a purpose-driven approach can instil, serving as both a compass and a source of inspiration during times of change and uncertainty.

Why does purpose play a crucial role in fostering team resilience?

As an example, let's consider a team within Unilever, the global consumer goods company, guided by the purpose "to make sustainable living commonplace." Unlike the fleeting allure of external rewards, intrinsic motivation draws strength from deep internal desires, values, and a profound sense of purpose. This exploration shows the synergy between purpose and intrinsic motivation, highlighting the impact of purpose as a guiding light that leads teams toward resilience. In this context, the team's purpose revolves around advancing Unilever's mission to promote sustainable living practices worldwide.

As the team works towards reducing environmental impact or developing sustainable product lines, purpose-driven work transcends isolated tasks, presenting itself as an integral part of a larger, purposeful journey. Intrinsic fulfilment becomes a powerful force propelling team members through difficulties, anchoring them in a sense of purpose beyond daily challenges. Connecting with Unilever's mission encourages a commitment to making sustainable living commonplace, acting as a secure foundation during challenging times. Integrating intrinsic motivation with ownership and autonomy leads to a proactive response to challenges. For instance, team members may actively engage in initiatives such as reducing carbon emissions or implementing eco-friendly packaging, driven by a belief in Unilever's purpose, and desire to see that fulfilled.

Unilever's purpose sparks emotional investment, encouraging team members to be stewards of their contributions. This emotional connection becomes a source of resilience, motivating individuals to rise above adversity when faced with obstacles. For instance, encountering supply chain disruptions or market fluctuations prompts the team to use their emotional connections to Unilever's purpose, seeking innovative solutions and collaborative strategies to continue making sustainable living commonplace. Purpose-driven individuals see challenges as opportunities for development, viewing setbacks as valuable learning experiences contributing to personal and collective growth. This perspective often aligns with personal aspirations, reinforcing the team's commitment to Unilever's mission.

A north star

A purpose is the north star; it acts as a compass, directing individuals' actions and decisions, especially during stormy weather. The purpose is why people want to work together, collaborate, and achieve a shared goal. All parties come together around this one main reason for being. While core values are guardrails for how people make decisions and behave, the purpose defines the why. Teams are often busy delivering their work with little idea of why they're doing it – having a clear purpose increases motivation and engagement.

Consider the example of the CEO whom I had the privilege of coaching during the challenging times brought about by the global pandemic. Faced with unprecedented uncertainties, this leader recognised the pivotal role of purpose in guiding their team through the storm. By articulating a team purpose that resonated with the values and aspirations of its members, they instilled a sense of meaning into the collective efforts. This purpose became a rallying point during the pandemic, aligning the team's energies toward a common objective.

The CEO's commitment to a team purpose proved instrumental in maintaining high motivation and resilience. Team members felt a stronger connection to their work, understanding not just what they were doing but why it mattered. This, in turn, created a subculture within the broader organisational context, where the team's purpose became a source of inspiration and cohesion. The experience of this CEO underscores the importance of not only having an overarching organisational purpose, but also crafting a distinct team purpose. While the company's purpose provides direction, a team purpose connects individuals with a profound sense of significance, fostering a deeper understanding of the collective "why." In essence, the strategic design of a team purpose unites team members in purposeful endeavours even during the most challenging circumstances.

During a recent workshop with a client's team, the power of uncovering their team's purpose became evident. Guiding them through a series of introspective exercises and discussions, the team came together around a shared purpose that supported their collective values and aspirations. Witnessing this process unfold was truly impactful, as team members transitioned from individual contributors to a united force with a common mission. The newfound clarity of purpose added a renewed sense of motivation and commitment within the team. The impact could be seen through their daily tasks, transforming routine activities into meaningful contributions towards a larger goal. Notably, the team's enhanced cohesion and intrinsic motivation translated into improved performance, innovation, and a shared sense of accomplishment. This experience showed how aligning a team with a purpose can create positive change, strengthening their collective resilience and propelling them towards sustained success.

Adaptability

Purpose-driven teams are inherently more inclined to embrace change and navigate uncertainties with resilience. The purpose acts as a guide, infusing every challenge with a sense of purpose that goes beyond the current obstacles. This, in turn, creates a culture where adaptability is not merely a reactive response but a proactive stance, a strategic tool used by teams to stay aligned with their greater mission. Teams, motivated by a shared sense of purpose, become hotbeds for creative thinking and problem-solving. The purpose acts as a catalyst, encouraging team members to explore novel ideas, challenge the status quo, and approach challenges with a fresh perspective. To conclude purpose not only inspires teams to weather change but also propels them to proactively shape their path amid uncertainties.

How to define your team/organisation's purpose:

Crafting purpose statements involves articulating the team's objectives and the positive influence it aspires to have. A particularly effective and easily facilitated method for formulating a team's purpose can be broken down into two parts.

Part 1 – Defining why the team exists:

» Defining your team's role:

Generate a concise sentence encapsulating the fundamental function or output of your team. Encourage team members to contribute multiple ideas, group them based on commonalities, and rank them in order of significance. If your team engages in diverse activities, try to distil a unifying concept that best represents the majority of your work. For instance, "We streamline supply chain processes to ensure timely and efficient product delivery" or "We provide personalised financial consulting to help clients achieve their financial goals."

» Identifying our key stakeholders:

List the various groups or stakeholders your team serves and pinpoint the primary one. Specify whether your assistance spans broadly across senior executives or is more department-specific, such as sales or marketing. Clarify if your focus is on a particular department or the entire organisation.

» Envisioning impact:

Explore the purpose of your team by understanding the challenges and benefits experienced by your primary stakeholders. Explore how your team can contribute to their success and, most crucially, articulate the ultimate impact you aim to achieve in their lives, extending beyond functional contributions. For instance, "Empowering our managers to lead with confidence" or "Equipping advisors to elevate client satisfaction."

Part 2 – Write your team purpose statement:

Formulate a statement based on "Our team (insert what you do) to/for (insert specific audience) so that (insert intended impact)."

» Examples of purpose statements:

"Our team streamlines the food manufacturing supply chain for the timely delivery of quality products, ensuring a seamless and reliable food supply chain."

"We create compelling marketing content to guide individuals in navigating the complexities of wealth management, fostering financial literacy and confidence."

» Does everyone understand the purpose?

In the pursuit of establishing a purpose-driven team or organisation, effective communication and strategic alignment serve as foundational principles. From products and services to cultural elements and decision-making processes, every operational dimension should align with and contribute to the team or organisational purpose.

Tracy Aust, Principal at West Thames College, emphasises the importance of a shared goal and a common purpose that is understood by all team members. She also underscores the significance of trust, confidence, and diversity within the team, including those who may challenge or offer different perspectives, stating, "I think the whole aspect of having a shared goal and a common purpose that's understood by all is vital." This alignment establishes the groundwork for constructing a purpose-driven framework, ensuring that the entirety of your team or organisation functions in sync with its core mission.

Engaging employees in the purpose journey is equally vital. Developing a sense of ownership empowers them to actively contribute, increasing not just productivity but also levels of motivation, commitment, and job satisfaction. Communication becomes a linchpin in this process—sharing the purpose with clarity with internal and external stakeholders. Using effective communication tools such as messaging, storytelling, and branding authenticates the purpose, creating a narrative that resonates with all involved. To truly measure the impact of a purpose-driven approach, robust mechanisms must be in place. Transparently communicating the outcomes of purpose-driven initiatives to stakeholders becomes an ongoing responsibility.

Lastly, the journey towards purpose is dynamic, requiring continuous evaluation and adaptation. Regular reviews ensure that the purpose aligns with evolving goals, values, and the external environment. Being open to necessary adjustments guarantees that the purpose remains not only relevant but also impactful and meaningful over time. Following these steps paves the way for a purpose-driven team or organisation that integrates its mission into its daily operations and culture.

It's important to recognise that not everyone's purpose aligns perfectly with the organisation. However, this process can bring clarity regarding the significance of their career and the company they choose to work for. When there's a broader alignment between personal and organisational purposes, it leads to heightened employee engagement. Encouraging this exploration not only contributes to the individual growth of employees but also strengthens the overall connection between individuals and the organisation.

Chapter summary

This chapter explores the concept of purpose-driven organisations and teams, emphasising the significance of having a clear and compelling purpose that goes beyond profit maximisation. It provides real-world examples and highlights the role of purpose in fostering team resilience, intrinsic motivation, cohesion, and adaptability. The chapter outlines a practical approach to defining a team's purpose, stressing the importance of effective communication, strategic alignment, and encouraging a sense of ownership among employees. Additionally, it underscores the value of encouraging employees to explore and align their purposes with the organisation's purpose, leading to heightened engagement and a stronger connection between individuals and the collective mission.

Reflection

How would you articulate your sense of purpose in your personal and professional life?

Reflect on a pivotal moment when your understanding of your purpose evolved. What did you learn about yourself?

Does your current workplace have a clearly defined purpose? How well do you think it aligns with your values and goals?

Reflect on a challenging period in your professional life. How did a sense of purpose or lack thereof impact your resilience and ability to navigate difficulties?

If you are in a leadership position, how have you or could you use your team's shared purpose to guide them during challenging times?

Can you think of specific actions or initiatives that could enhance a purpose-driven culture in your workplace?

Have you actively thought about your employees' or colleagues' individual purposes? How might understanding and supporting these individual purposes contribute to a more engaged and motivated team?

What resources or initiatives could your organisation provide to help employees discover and align with their purpose?

Do you feel a personal alignment between your purpose and the purpose of your organisation or team? If not, how might you seek or create alignment?

In your leadership role, how do you ensure that the organisation's purpose remains relevant and impactful over time?

Action

Craft a personal purpose statement that reflects your values, aspirations, and the impact you want to make in your personal and professional life.

Evaluate how well your current workplace aligns with your purpose. If there's misalignment, consider initiating a conversation with leadership to explore ways to better integrate personal and organisational purposes.

Propose or organise a team workshop to revisit and redefine the team's purpose. Discuss how the shared purpose can be a source of resilience during challenging times.

Initiate conversations with colleagues or team members about their purposes. Encourage open dialogue about personal aspirations and explore ways to align these with team and organisational goals.

Demonstrate your commitment to the team's purpose through your actions and decision-making. Be a role model for how purpose-driven leadership looks in practice.

If you're in a leadership position, prioritise leadership development programs that emphasise the role of purpose in guiding decisions, fostering resilience, and inspiring teams.

CHAPTER TWO:
CREATING RESILIENT PROCESSES

What you will gain from this chapter

An understanding of the three key stages - Reduce, Regulate, and Repair - that resilient teams incorporate to build and maintain resilience.

Insights into the importance of proactive scenario planning and strategic preparedness in minimising potential challenges and disruptions.

Knowledge of how to effectively manage and navigate through crises in real time, using case studies and personal experiences as examples.

Strategies for creating a culture of continuous improvement and learning from setbacks through structured debriefing processes.

An appreciation for the role of clear communication, collaboration, and emotional well-being in building team resilience.

Insight: Processes that serve you to build team resilience

During a coaching session with the rowers preparing to circumnavigate Great Britain, I facilitated a visualisation exercise. As we talked about the details of setting up a para-anchor—a maritime tool resembling a parachute—team members immersed themselves in mentally navigating the process. The para-anchor, deployed from a boat's stern, serves as a vital component during challenging conditions, such as storms, by creating drag in the water to stabilise and decelerate the boat.

However, the exercise went beyond a straightforward walkthrough. I prompted each rower to not only envision the successful deployment of the para-anchor but also explore potential pitfalls and complications that might arise. This added layer of visualisation helped create a proactive and resilient mindset within the team. By encouraging the rowers to identify and discuss potential challenges, they engaged in a form of scenario planning. In the ensuing discussions, team members openly shared their scenarios, creating a diverse range of challenges to consider with the para-anchor.

This collaborative process allowed the team to anticipate obstacles collectively and, more importantly, to develop mitigation strategies as a team. It became a dynamic exercise where the rowers not only visualised success but also confronted and prepared for potential setbacks, instilling a robust process within their teamwork. This exercise, rooted in visualisation and scenario planning, played an important role in shaping the team's resilient approach to challenges they might encounter during their ambitious journey around Great Britain.

Establishing resilient processes is crucial for the long-term success and sustainability of a team. In today's dynamic landscape, where markets, technologies, and consumer preferences evolve rapidly, resilient processes enable teams to adapt swiftly to changes in the business environment, ensuring agility without compromising efficiency. By anticipating potential challenges and risks through strategic planning, resilient processes act as a shield against unexpected disruptions, allowing teams to identify, assess, and mitigate risks proactively, reducing the likelihood of adverse impacts on operations and performance.

Well-defined processes contribute to operational efficiency by streamlining workflows, eliminating bottlenecks, and enhancing the overall effectiveness of daily operations, which becomes particularly crucial during challenging times. Resilient processes also help create a culture of continuous improvement through regular assessments and adjustments based on lessons learned from challenges, contributing to the organisation's overall growth and allowing for the refinement of processes over time.

Moreover, resilient processes create a sense of security and stability, positively impacting employee morale and well-being, as employees thrive in environments where they feel supported and confident in the team's ability to handle challenges. Knowing that there are established procedures for overcoming obstacles can alleviate stress and enhance job satisfaction. Ultimately, organisations and teams that invest in resilient processes are better positioned for long-term sustainability, as the ability to weather storms, adapt to changing circumstances, and learn from experiences ensures that the organisation can endure and thrive in a competitive and unpredictable business landscape.

There are three key stages I incorporate into a team to ensure that they are building a resilient team: Reduce, Regulate, and Repair. These stages encapsulate a holistic approach to building and sustaining resilience, providing a structured framework for individuals and teams to thrive in the face of challenges.

The first stage, "Reduce," centres on proactive measures aimed at minimising potential stressors and adverse conditions. It involves strategic planning, forward-thinking, and scenario analysis to identify and mitigate risks before they escalate. By implementing preventive strategies and encouraging a culture of preparedness, this stage sets the foundation for resilient individuals and teams.

Moving to the second stage, "Regulate," the focus shifts to managing stressors and challenges that inevitably arise. Here, individuals and teams develop effective coping mechanisms, emotional regulation skills, and adaptive strategies to navigate through adversity. The goal is not just to endure challenges but to maintain a sense of balance, composure, and well-being in the face of uncertainty.

The final stage, "Repair," acknowledges that setbacks and challenges are an inherent part of any journey. In this stage, the emphasis is on learning from experiences, adapting to change, and recovering from setbacks. It involves reflection, feedback, and continuous improvement, developing a mindset of resilience that not only bounces back from adversity but also thrives through the transformative power of learning and growth. Together, these three stages form a dynamic process, offering a roadmap for individuals and teams to build, sustain, and continually enhance their resilience.

The Reduce Process

The rowing team example I gave at the beginning of this chapter is an excellent illustration of scenario planning, a part of the "reduce" phase of the process. First, to lessen the impact of obstacles, resilient teams take a proactive approach to addressing them. They use predictive techniques, recognising previous setbacks that affected their output and actively looking for possible roadblocks in the future, such as an impending increase in workload. Through meticulous planning and contingency preparation, these teams ensure they are well-equipped to face upcoming challenges. This proactive stance often involves engaging in "what-if" discussions to simulate likely or high-risk scenarios. Drawing a parallel, the significance of such preparatory measures is highlighted by historical events like the Titanic disaster, where iceberg warning drills and "what-if" disaster scenario reviews could have potentially saved lives.

I worked for 20 years in the food industry, where resilient teams take a proactive approach to lessen problems by foreseeing and preparing for possible interruptions. For example, a team producing food might foresee any disruptions in the supply chain or changes in consumer preferences by analysing past data and industry patterns. This forward-thinking approach allows them to identify potential "icebergs" such as ingredient shortages, regulatory changes, or unexpected shifts in market demand.

Drawing inspiration from industries like logistics and supply chain management, where anticipating and mitigating disruptions is paramount, food industry teams implement strategies such as diversifying suppliers, maintaining strategic stockpiles, and regularly updating their production processes to ensure adaptability to unforeseen circumstances. By conducting regular reviews and scenario planning, they equip themselves with the tools needed to navigate challenges and maintain a resilient stance in the face of dynamic industry conditions.

Jim Hotaling, Global Head of Leadership Development at N2Growth and former Command Chief of the US Air Force, echoed the importance of scenario planning in bolstering resilience. By drawing parallels between military training and organisational planning, he emphasised the need for proactive readiness in the face of diverse challenges. Hotaling cited Special Operations as a compelling example, highlighting the lower levels of post-traumatic stress among special operation forces compared to regular forces. He attributed this difference to the rigorous training and thorough preparation undergone by special forces, ultimately resulting in heightened resilience when confronted with challenging situations.

Amid the energy and the cost-of-living crisis in the UK in 2022, one of my clients grew increasingly concerned about the unfolding situation. To address these concerns and strengthen resilience within the team, we engaged in a strategic exercise designed to explore various scenarios and potential challenges. The exercise involved envisioning hypothetical situations such as a 20% loss in sales, a 25% increase in operational costs, and contingencies for scenarios like prolonged recruitment processes or unexpected departures.

While this approach may initially appear pessimistic, it serves as an effective strategy for proactive resilience building. By exploring "what if" scenarios, the team embarked on a comprehensive exploration of potential challenges, enabling them to formulate proactive and strategic mitigations. This not only resulted in a set of well-thought-out strategies but also established a team-oriented process for addressing difficulties as they arose. The exercise provided a foundation for collaborative problem-solving and equipped the team with a mindset ready to navigate unforeseen challenges, fostering adaptability and resilience in the face of uncertainties.

This proactive approach to scenario planning proved instrumental during a period of economic turbulence. By considering a range of potential challenges, from fluctuations in sales to increased operational costs, the team not only developed resilience but also cultivated a sense of preparedness. The "what if" exercise facilitated an open dialogue within the team, encouraging members to share insights and diverse perspectives on navigating these challenges.

Moreover, the process went beyond creating theoretical scenarios; it involved the team in devising concrete and actionable mitigating strategies. Each hypothetical challenge became an opportunity for the team to brainstorm, strategize, and build a collective understanding of how to respond effectively. In doing so, the team developed a shared language and approach for addressing uncertainties, creating a culture of adaptability and cooperation.

As the team considered different scenarios, they not only fortified their resilience in the face of known challenges but also gained valuable experience in collaborative problem-solving. This empowered them to confront unforeseen obstacles with a proactive and cohesive mindset, ensuring that they could navigate the complexities of the evolving situation. The exercise, initially perceived as a doomsday approach, transformed into a cornerstone for building a resilient team capable of thriving amid uncertainties.

Recognising preparedness from a personal standpoint is another activity that resilient teams undertake. Knowing everyone's present state allows us to determine which members of the team need to take a break and handle fewer tasks, while others are in a high-capacity mode and can handle more team challenges. To increase the team's overall resilience, it is important to understand this. The nature of the team and the activities they are involved in will greatly influence how dynamic and real-time this process is in the given situation. For example, the rowers I coached made it a habit to eat and spend time together during breakfast, lunch, and dinner. They developed a simple 3-point check-in system to use at each of these daily meals. A brief update was given regarding the day's focus, objectives and challenges including destination focus, celebrations of progress so far, and any potential difficulties caused by the tides, weather, or shipping lanes. Crucially, each rower would share their current state on a scale of 1 to 5, where 1 would indicate they are feeling weak, fatigued, hungry, or seasick and are having difficulty rowing, and 5 would indicate they are on top form and strong. With everyone knowing where the other members were, the team was able to modify the day's activities according to individual capabilities after each member shared their scale number and a brief explanation of the situation.

A different kind of check-in is the Personal Professional Check-In (PPC), which was utilised by CVS Health. CVS Health ensures they do a brief PPC at the beginning of any interaction, whether they're opening a meeting or simply catching up over the phone with someone they haven't spoken to in a few days, by asking the following two questions:

What personal struggles are you facing?

What aspects of your job are you finding difficult?

These check-ins were used by CVS Health's chief information officer, Roshan Navagamuwa, with his staff under a period of intense pressure as they worked with a new CEO against the backdrop of CVS and Aetna merging. He stated the exercises "opened up a level of shared commitment" to the team's new mission. These intentional inquiries aimed to create a shared commitment within the team, emphasising the importance of a psychologically safe environment for genuine and open responses, as discussed in the dedicated chapter on this topic.

When building on the foundation of the psychologically safe environment you have cultivated, it is important for team members to proactively identify early warning signs of potential challenges. Beyond mere encouragement, instil a proactive mindset among your team to openly communicate their concerns and provide timely alerts. This not only promotes a culture of transparency but also empowers individuals to share insights that could prevent or mitigate issues before they escalate. For instance, consider a sales team navigating a dynamic market. In this context, team members might encounter shifts in customer preferences, emerging market trends, or evolving competitor strategies. The team leader can gain valuable insights by fostering an environment where individuals feel comfortable expressing their observations and concerns. This proactive communication can lead to strategic adjustments, targeted interventions, or innovative solutions, ultimately enhancing the team's adaptability and resilience in a competitive sales landscape.

Drawing from personal experience, I understand the important role of creating an environment where team members can promptly share any concerns. In a leadership position I once held, I oversaw a team that was involved in a new product launch to the UK retail market. I emphasised the importance of immediate feedback from any retailer presentations. While positive responses were anticipated, negative feedback or concerns from the retailer were equally valuable. I encouraged my team to share these concerns promptly, recognising that such insights served as learning opportunities for our collective growth. This transparent feedback loop not only contributed to the refinement of our approach with other retailers but also became an integral part of the ongoing "repair" process within the team.

It's common to approach organisational policies with scepticism, but it's essential to understand their underlying purpose and significance. As a trustee of Chichester District Foodbank, I have come to appreciate that well-defined policies and robust governance are fundamental to its smooth operation. Instead of viewing policies as restrictive, consider them as Standard Operating Procedures (SOPs), which helps integrate them seamlessly into the team's and organisation's modus operandi. Within the charity I serve, an array of policies contributes to its well-functioning. One of these policies is one on the important matter of safeguarding. This crucial policy meticulously outlines procedures and protocols, ensuring the welfare and protection of individuals associated with the charity. It goes beyond a mere formality, symbolising the organisation's dedication to maintaining a secure and ethical working environment. The safeguarding policy serves as a proactive measure, emphasising prevention and preparedness to safeguard the values and integrity of the organisation.

While having the policy is crucial, the real efficacy lies in the adherence to the procedures laid out. In the context of safeguarding, the SOP delineates who to contact when a safeguarding issue arises, the reporting mechanisms, internal information-sharing protocols, and the process of collaborating with external entities such as the police, social services, or regulators if needed. Establishing and following this comprehensive procedure empowers individuals to act swiftly and decisively when issues arise, providing a clear and effective framework for the team to navigate challenges, especially in sensitive areas like safeguarding.

The Reduce process stands at the core of resilient teams, providing a strategic and forward-thinking approach to address challenges. It goes beyond mere preparedness, developing a proactive mindset that turns potential obstacles into opportunities for growth and innovation. Through scenario planning exercises, resilient teams recognise the importance of anticipating and mitigating disruptions. They take inspiration from various industries, highlighting the need to identify potential challenges like market shifts, supply chain disruptions, or regulatory changes. The Reduce process becomes a philosophy ingrained in the team's approach, enabling them to thrive amid uncertainties and emerge stronger in the face of change.

Moreover, the Reduce process goes beyond theoretical considerations by actively involving teams in devising concrete and actionable strategies. This collaborative problem-solving not only fortifies resilience but also creates a shared language and approach to addressing uncertainties. The proactive stance creates a culture of continuous learning and innovation, where challenges are not merely endured but embraced as opportunities for improvement.

In essence, the Reduce process isn't just a strategic exercise; it's a mindset that permeates the team's approach to challenges. It encourages a dynamic and real-time evaluation of potential disruptions, enabling teams to stay ahead in an ever-evolving landscape. As teams engage in scenario planning, conduct drills, and encourage proactive thinking, they not only build resilience but also cultivate a spirit of resilience that becomes ingrained in their way of working. The Reduce process is not just a process in resilience-building; it's a philosophy that propels teams to thrive amid uncertainties and complexities, ensuring they emerge stronger and more adaptable in the face of change.

The Regulate Process

Navigating through challenging circumstances is an inevitable part of any team's journey, requiring strategic management in real time. This part of the process is how you respond and manage those difficult scenarios when they come up. Often these can be situations that you did not even think could happen, and if you did then you are at a distinct advantage. As I reflect on the challenging period of leading a commercial team for a yoghurt manufacturing business, the unforeseen strike in our French factory stands out as a defining moment. Our operations, meticulously managed with robust processes, faced an unexpected disruption when the French factory staff initiated a strike over pay. With all production centralised in France, this labour dispute sent shockwaves through our supply chain, impacting our ability to deliver yoghurt to the UK retail market. During this crisis, I found myself at the helm, navigating uncharted waters without prior experience in crisis management. The urgency of the situation demanded a swift and comprehensive assessment.

Collaborating closely with the supply chain team, we examined our stock management systems, analysing the available stock by product line and forecasting customer demand. This initial evaluation revealed the pressing need for a strategic allocation of stock, a critical step in mitigating the potential fallout from the strike. Recognising that effective communication was paramount, I instituted daily meetings involving both the supply chain and sales teams. These sessions became a vital forum for sharing real-time updates on the evolving situation in France, brainstorming allocation strategies, and identifying potential out-of-stock items.

To empower the sales team in their customer interactions, I ensured they were well-versed in the ongoing challenges and the steps we were taking to address them. This proactive communication extended beyond internal teams, with personalised phone calls with the retailer category directors and also face-to-face meetings with key customers. Simultaneously, my interactions with the French management team were characterised by transparency and clarity regarding the situation in the UK. I conveyed the gravity of our challenges, emphasising the potential harm to our brand and the financial implications, creating a shared understanding of the severity of the situation.

While the resolution of the strike after 3 weeks marked a turning point, the aftermath presented ongoing challenges, with stock shortages persisting for an additional 4-5 weeks. This period demanded sustained daily meetings, continued communication strategies, and proactive crisis resolution efforts. The experience has become an integral part of my leadership journey, shaping my approach to crisis management and reinforcing the need for a proactive and resilient team culture capable of weathering unforeseen storms.

The lessons drawn from the challenging scenario of managing a team during the strike in the French factory highlight the key aspects of the 'regulate' process - in essence, how you manage when there is a crisis or challenge within your organisation. Firstly, in a crisis, the ability to assess the situation swiftly, honestly and accurately is crucial for teams. Collaborative efforts across organisational departments ensure a comprehensive understanding, with each team or organisational member contributing unique insights. This collective intelligence considers internal capabilities, external dependencies, and potential impacts. The assessment extends to resource evaluation, guiding strategic resource allocation. Understanding the crisis' potential impact on operations allows teams to anticipate challenges and make informed decisions. Rapid decision-making is facilitated by clear communication channels. Overall, this holistic assessment lays the groundwork for effective crisis resolution.

Secondly, strategic resource allocation is important, irrespective of the industry or context. To effectively manage unexpected disruptions, organisations must carefully assess the current situation, forecast future needs, and prioritise resource allocation based on critical requirements. This process begins with a thorough analysis of available resources, categorising and quantifying what is available. This comprehensive understanding forms the basis for informed decision-making.

Forecasting involves looking ahead and using historical data and trends to predict future needs and potential fluctuations. This proactive stance allows teams to prepare for anticipated challenges. By prioritising resource allocation according to essential needs, organisations can develop a targeted and effective response strategy. Aligning resource distribution with specific requirements enables teams to optimise their crisis response, improving efficiency and minimising negative impacts. This strategic approach to resource management is universally applicable across various fields and forms a cornerstone of resilient crisis management. By adopting this method, organisations can better navigate unexpected disruptions, maintain operational continuity, and emerge stronger from challenging situations.

Thirdly, clear communication is vital for successfully overcoming challenges across all industries and situations. It forms the backbone of effective crisis management. Regular, open communication, both within the organisation and externally, is crucial. Internally, it aligns team members, ensuring everyone understands the challenges and can work together to navigate uncertain times. Externally, transparent communication builds trust with stakeholders by keeping them informed about steps being taken to address the crisis. Teams should also be prepared to engage with customers during difficult periods. This involves explaining ongoing challenges, outlining strategies to mitigate issues, and detailing potential impacts on services. By equipping teams for these interactions, organisations ensure their representatives can provide accurate information, address concerns, and proactively manage client expectations. This approach underscores the importance of communication at all levels, forming a key component of resilient crisis management strategies.

Fourthly, open and honest communication is important when dealing with senior management or external partners. It helps convey the true extent of challenges, ensuring all key players understand the situation accurately. This approach allows teams to collaboratively tackle issues, foresee potential outcomes, and develop preventive strategies. It fosters a sense of shared responsibility and dedication among all involved. Whether facing supply chain disruptions, labour disputes, or other crises, transparency is essential for building resilience. These interactions are collaborative efforts to navigate difficulties, align goals, and secure mutual commitment to overcoming the crisis. This experience highlights the need for a resilient team culture that embraces flexibility and values effective communication. It demonstrates the team's capacity not just to survive unexpected challenges, but to learn and emerge stronger from them. During crises, it's vital to maintain focus on the team or organisation's overall purpose and mission.

Reflecting on my experience dealing with the French strike, I recognise a missed opportunity in not employing this approach. The crisis revealed a critical oversight: the lack of a clear organisational purpose. This became evident when compared to the example in the previous chapter (Creating team/organisational purpose), where a CEO effectively used their organisation's purpose to guide decisions during the pandemic. This contrast highlights how a well-defined purpose can provide direction and motivation during challenging times, keeping teams focused and aligned.

This allowed the team to gain clarity amidst chaos, effectively managing emotions and helping them switch from a "survival" to a "thriving" mindset. The act of pausing to lift their gaze from the immediate challenges enabled them to identify opportunities and solutions. In hindsight, my key reflection and learning from the French strike experience underscore the importance of having a well-defined purpose and mission for the organisation. Using this purpose as a reference throughout the crisis would have provided direction and resilience during the strike.

During a crisis or challenging period, the emotional well-being of the team is also an important component of effective leadership. Leaders must recognise the impact of emotions on team dynamics and performance. In the forthcoming chapter on leadership, we will explore strategies for developing resilience within the team by addressing emotions, providing support, and creating a positive and constructive environment. Managing emotions involves not only acknowledging the challenges but also guiding the team in a way that promotes a sense of stability and confidence. By understanding the emotional pulse of the team, leaders can implement strategies to boost morale, encourage open communication, and cultivate a collective mindset focused on overcoming challenges. This proactive approach to emotional management is integral to building a resilient team capable of navigating uncertainties with cohesion and adaptability.

As my experiences broadened, I have learnt new techniques for guiding teams through challenging periods, whether triggered by the loss of a substantial customer or a senior leader leaving the organisation. Such situations introduce an element of uncertainty and change, demanding creative solutions for effective navigation. I've previously emphasised the significance of returning to the organisation's purpose or mission statement - another valuable approach involves what might seem like a cliché but proves effective: "flipping the script." This method entails reframing challenges as opportunities, encouraging a shift in perspective that opens new possibilities and encourages a proactive mindset within the team. By incorporating these strategies, teams can cultivate resilience and adaptability, transforming adversity into a catalyst for growth and innovation. If you would like to facilitate this process yourself as a team leader, here is the approach:

Transforming challenges into opportunities: This interactive session aims to fuel creativity and develop positive problem-solving skills with your team.

Firstly, encourage each team member to reflect and share the challenges they currently face as a team, initiating an open conversation.

Next, share the identified challenge on a screen or flip chart. Prompt the team to collectively reframe the challenge by posing the question, "What opportunity does this challenge present for our team or organisation?" This transformative step redirects the perspective, shifting from perceiving challenges as obstacles to viewing them as potential opportunities, cultivating a broader and more positive mindset.

Generate a comprehensive list of potential opportunities or solutions arising from the reframed challenge.

Prioritise and rank these opportunities based on their perceived impact.

Facilitate a thorough discussion to review and refine the identified opportunities.

Conclude the session by reaching a consensus on the proposed solution to be actively pursued by the team.

In conclusion, the Regulate Process is a critical stage for teams navigating challenges. My experience during a factory strike highlights the importance of swift assessments, strategic resource allocation, and effective communication. These principles are universal across industries, emphasising the need for a resilient team culture. Maintaining a connection to the organisational purpose is crucial during crises, as it provides direction and resilience. Broadening experiences reveal techniques like "flipping the script" for turning challenges into opportunities. The Regulate Process is pivotal for fostering resilience and innovation. It guides teams to proactively manage crises, transforming obstacles into avenues for growth.

The Repair Process

Consider the French yoghurt plant strike that I mentioned previously as an illustration. The strike disrupted the supply chain, making it harder for the company to provide products to stores in the UK. It also did a lot of damage to the company's finances and brand, as well as to the supply chain and sales team. In the immediate aftermath of resolving the strike and stabilising operations, we quickly resumed normal activities without taking time to reflect on the experience. The company's focus shifted back to meeting production targets, managing orders, and ensuring a seamless supply chain in order to supply the UK marketplace. However, by not pausing for reflection, we missed an opportunity to explore deeper into the root causes of the labour strike. We did not explore whether there were warning signs or communication gaps that could have been addressed earlier.

We also didn't assess the resilience of our supply chain and whether there were opportunities for improvement. The absence of a reflective process meant that we continued with its operations without incorporating the lessons learned from the French strike. A reflective analysis could have revealed insights into enhancing communication channels, implementing proactive labour relations strategies, and diversifying production locations to mitigate the impact of future strikes or similar disruptions. The Repair process entails overcoming stress, picking up lessons from mistakes, and making appropriate adjustments.

In the early days of the pandemic, in March 2020, when the "stay at home" orders were put into effect, organisations all over the world suffered. This sudden change caused strong feelings, daily meetings to talk things over, and a strong desire to quickly come up with ways to deal with the unique problems that the lockdowns caused. Every organisation had a hard time adjusting to the new situation, and teams worked nonstop to figure out how to best face and solve the complex problems that were coming up on many fronts. As the weeks turned into months, there was a big change in businesses around the world. Over time, the intense crisis mode started to fade away, giving way to what became known as the "new normal." This marked the change from crisis mode to the repair phase, during which businesses tried to get back to normal while still facing problems. In the repair phase, resilient teams are very aware of how things are changing and are trying to go back to routine and have a sense of control. The phrase "new normal" refers to more than just a change in circumstances. It also refers to a general acceptance that the immediate disaster or challenge is over and a new way of doing things is taking shape. It means that teams need to stop making decisions based on emergencies and start making decisions in a more measured and flexible way. For teams to be resilient, they need to recognise this important shift. It means realising that the strong emotional and strategic reactions that are needed in a crisis may not be as important now. Teams should instead focus on knowing how things have changed, figuring out how their operations fit into the new situation, and accepting the "new normal" as a whole. The repair phase needs team members to be aware of many things and to understand them all. This shared understanding is very important because it creates a way for everyone to work together to deal with recurring problems. This makes the team stronger and more flexible. Being able to switch from crisis mode to repair mode shows how resilient the team is and how well it can adapt to changes in the outside world.

Following proactive measures, resilient teams prioritise debriefing meetings, often referred to as "after-action reviews." Paul Randall, Strategic Advisor for Creditinfo Group, underscores the significance of collective learning and debriefing in team development. Reflecting on experiences, evaluating successes and failures, and using these insights for adaptation and improvement are integral to enhancing team resilience. The U.S. Armed Forces have effectively implemented debriefings for three decades, proving them to be a highly effective method for team development. A debrief is when a team reflects on the successes and mistakes of a recent project or challenge, learns from them, and makes plans for future projects that they can carry out. Debriefings work best when they allow team members to talk freely with each other, creating an atmosphere where ideas can be shared openly. Because of this, important information comes to light that might not have been found any other way. According to research, teams who carry out debriefs regularly perform better than teams who do not. On average, their performance goes up between 20% to 25% (Tannenbaum and Cerasoli, 2013).

Resilience lies at the heart of adaptability, the ability to transform and adjust in the face of challenges. It allows us to learn and, at times, unlearn, paving the way for continuous progress. In this journey of resilience, debriefing emerges as a crucial element. It acts as a haven for learning moments within the team, that serves as a compass for future development. Picture debriefing as a team huddle after a game, where we dissect the plays, celebrate the victories and discuss areas for improvement. It's our collective opportunity to reflect on what worked well and what didn't during our challenges. By sharing experiences, we create a wealth of insights that propel us forward. The essence of debriefing is to distil these insights into actionable plans, ensuring that each hurdle becomes a stepping stone towards growth. In simpler terms, debriefing is our team's special space for open conversations, learning from both successes and setbacks and gearing up for whatever comes next. It's our training ground for resilience—a place where we fine-tune our strategies, strengthen our unity and emerge even more robust as a team.

How to lead a debrief session?

Begin by creating a space where team members feel safe to express their thoughts openly. Emphasise the collective goal of learning and improvement, setting a tone for an honest conversation. As team members reflect on recent challenges, encourage them to share what went well and areas that could be enhanced. This initial discussion provides valuable insights into the team's dynamics and performance. Following the reflection phase, explore individual perspectives, allowing team members to express their unique observations and lessons learned. This step encourages diverse insights, contributing to a comprehensive understanding of the situation. Transition into brainstorming actionable plans for the future, focusing on strategies to use strengths and address weaknesses. Facilitate a consensus-building discussion to ensure alignment on proposed strategies and commitments. Finally, document key takeaways, actionable items, and commitments, creating a valuable reference for continuous improvement. This debriefing process not only enhances team resilience but also creates a culture of shared learning and growth.

Next, it is important to take the learnings from the debriefing session and incorporate them into the team and processes as appropriate. Another example from my career is when we faced a sudden disruption in the supply of a key ingredient due to unforeseen circumstances, impacting our production schedule and resulting in a short supply of a product to the customer. During the debriefing process, the team acknowledged the challenge of not having a backup supplier for a critical ingredient of the product that we were supplying. Therefore, in response, we adjusted our procurement processes to identify and establish relationships with alternative suppliers of this critical ingredient. This adaptive measure not only addressed a specific risk point but also fortified the team's resilience against similar challenges in the future. Moreover, throughout the debriefing session, the team recognised that communication breakdowns had occurred between the production and procurement departments during the crisis. To repair this, we implemented regular cross-departmental meetings and established clear communication channels to encourage collaboration. External relationships with suppliers were repaired through open dialogue and renegotiation of terms, ensuring a more robust network. By actively addressing concerns and making strategic adjustments, we not only recovered from the immediate challenge but also fortified our resilience for subsequent disruptions.

Recognition and acknowledgement are fundamental human needs, and during the aftermath of challenges, the repair phase for resilient teams is very important. At this point, the significance of appreciation takes centre stage, helping to guide the team toward recovery. At its core, appreciation serves to raise team morale and acknowledge the collective and individual efforts that led to navigating through adversity. By taking the time to express gratitude for the hard work, dedication, and resilience demonstrated by team members, leaders create a positive atmosphere that fuels a sense of accomplishment. Moreover, appreciation contributes significantly to rebuilding team cohesion, acting as a binding force that unites individuals under a shared sense of achievement.

The acknowledgement of individual strengths and collective accomplishments helps in rebuilding trust, ensuring a positive team culture, and reinforcing a spirit of solidarity. Additionally, in the repair phase, expressing appreciation becomes a motivational driver. It encourages team members to stay committed and engaged in the repair process. By highlighting the positive aspects of the team's response to challenges, leaders inspire a continued dedication to improvement and growth. Overall, appreciation acts as a catalyst for positive change, shaping the team's mindset and paving the way for a resilient and cohesive future. Recognising and expressing appreciation is a key element, and how we do it holds significance. Through public acknowledgement of both individual and collective contributions, organising celebratory events, and providing personalised thank-you notes, teams can foster a positive and collaborative culture. Creating opportunities for feedback and growth, acknowledging sacrifices made, and utilising recognition platforms contribute to creating a sense of accomplishment and shared success. Leadership visibility when expressing gratitude sets the tone for appreciating resilience and encouraging peer-to-peer recognition, ultimately strengthening interpersonal bonds.

Chapter summary

In this chapter, we explored the three vital stages essential for resilient teams to cultivate and uphold resilience: Reduce, Regulate, and Repair. The Reduce stage involves proactive measures aimed at minimising potential stressors and adverse conditions through strategic planning, scenario analysis, and developing a culture of preparedness. The Regulate stage focuses on effectively managing stressors and challenges as they arise, emphasising the use of coping mechanisms, emotional regulation skills, and adaptive strategies to navigate adversity while maintaining equilibrium and well-being. Lastly, the Repair stage underscores the significance of learning from setbacks, adapting to change, and rebounding from challenges through reflection, debriefing, and continuous improvement. This stage develops a resilient mindset that not only bounces back from adversity but also flourishes through the transformative process of learning and growth. By integrating these interconnected stages, teams can develop a comprehensive and dynamic approach to building and sustaining resilience in the face of ever-changing challenges.

Reflection

What strategies can you implement to create a culture of strategic preparedness within your team?

How can proactive scenario planning be integrated into your regular team practices and mindset?

Reflect on a past crisis. How did your team manage stressors and navigate through challenges in real time?

What improvements can be made to enhance your team's ability to maintain composure and collaborate effectively during crises?

Think about a recent project or challenge. How did your team benefit from the debriefing process in terms of learning and improvement?

What ongoing initiatives can be implemented to proactively address communication challenges within your team?

Action

Implement regular scenario planning sessions involving the entire team to identify potential challenges and opportunities.

Establish a cross-functional task force responsible for continuously evaluating and updating the team's strategic preparedness initiatives.

Implement a communication protocol that ensures swift and clear information flow during crises, defining roles and responsibilities.

Establish a culture of cooperation in the decision-making process by scheduling frequent meetings amongst departments to talk over current issues and possible fixes.

Formalise a structured debriefing process after the completion of each project or crisis, ensuring it becomes an integral part of the team's routine.

Implement a feedback loop mechanism that encourages team members to provide insights on communication effectiveness and suggests improvements.

PART TWO
NURTURING INDIVIDUAL AND TEAM RESILIENCE

CHAPTER THREE:
CREATING PERSONAL RESILIENCE

What you will gain from this chapter

Insights into the importance of personal resilience and how it contributes to overall team resilience, recognising that each team member brings their whole self to the collective effort.

Understanding of the three-point strategy for building personal resilience: clarity of purpose, daily habits, and building a supportive community.

Practical guidance on discovering and articulating your purpose, and how a clear sense of purpose serves as a motivator, compass, source of optimism, and catalyst for self-awareness.

Knowledge of essential daily habits for resilience, including expressing gratitude, celebrating successes, engaging in reflection, practising mindfulness, and cold water immersion, along with strategies for incorporating these habits into your routine.

Appreciation for the vital role of community in developing personal resilience, including the benefits of emotional support, a sense of belonging, exposure to diverse perspectives, and collective strength in times of crisis, as well as tips for building a strong support network.

Insight: A three-point strategy

While the primary focus of this book centres around team resilience, you might find yourself wondering about the inclusion of a chapter dedicated to personal resilience. The rationale behind this decision lies in the acknowledgement that each team member contributes their complete self to the collective effort. Our personal experiences, strengths, and challenges shape our professional interactions within a team context.

Recognising that resilient leadership involves more than just professional prowess, it extends into understanding and strengthening the personal dimensions of each team member and the leader too. By exploring personal resilience, we aim to underscore the interconnectedness of our well-being with the overall resilience of the team. In essence, our resilience significantly influences our collaborative dynamics and overall team effectiveness. This chapter seeks to provide insights, strategies, and reflections to empower you to navigate challenges as professionals and as holistic contributors to a resilient team. Whilst an abundance of resources exists on the subject of personal resilience through various mediums such as books, podcast interviews, and blogs, in this chapter I aim to distil essential concepts, drawing from my experiences and observations, to contribute a fresh perspective to the existing body of knowledge. By providing a concise exploration of this topic, I hope to offer practical insights, actionable strategies, and a thoughtful reflection that compliments the existing wealth of knowledge you may have encountered.

Personal resilience involves establishing a framework that acts as a robust support system during moments of adversity, be they monumental challenges or minor setbacks. In the unpredictable landscape of our lives, both on a personal level and within the organisational realm, uncertainties abound. My approach to personal resilience is based on a three-point strategy, like the stability provided by a three-legged stool. The three elements of this resilience framework intertwine to create a comprehensive system that not only helps navigate challenges but also develops a proactive mindset for anticipating and managing unforeseen situations. Let's explore each of these in greater detail:

Clarity of purpose

Achieving personal resilience begins with a profound understanding of your purpose. This involves introspection to identify your values, goals, and overarching mission in life. When your purpose is crystal clear, it serves as a guiding light during difficult times, anchoring you and providing direction. In this section we will explore strategies for uncovering and articulating your purpose, emphasising its pivotal role in developing resilience.

Daily habits for resilience

Resilience is not solely a response to major adversities but is cultivated through daily practices. This element focuses on incorporating habits that fortify your mental, emotional, and physical well-being. From mindfulness routines and self-reflection exercises to healthy lifestyle choices, establishing a daily resilience routine becomes a cornerstone in navigating life's ups and downs. This section will provide practical insights into cultivating these habits and integrating them into your daily life.

Building a supportive community

The third element underscores the importance of cultivating a resilient community around you. Human connection and a robust support system are invaluable during challenging times. This section will explore strategies for building and maintaining meaningful personal and professional relationships. It emphasises the mutual support networks that contribute significantly to individual and collective resilience.

By examining and incorporating these three elements of resilience into your life, you can create a well-rounded approach to personal resilience.

Your Why (Purpose)

People have dedicated whole books on this topic such as Simon Sinek with his helpful book, Start with Why. Having a clearly defined sense of purpose stands as a cornerstone for cultivating personal resilience. Firstly, a well-articulated purpose serves as a powerful motivator, propelling individuals to overcome obstacles and persevere through adversity. It acts as an unwavering source of inspiration, providing a compelling reason to press forward even in the face of setbacks.

I vividly recall the onset of the pandemic, a time when its immediate impact reverberated through my coaching business. Engagements were cancelled, and promising proposals seemed to dissipate into thin air. Faced with a challenging outlook and dwindling motivation, I found myself at a significant point during a walk by the coast, which was my daily outdoor exercise during the pandemic. It was at this moment that I consciously revisited my purpose: to "unlock human potential, build growth strategies, and create resilient mindsets." This reaffirmation became a wellspring of inspiration. It prompted profound questions: "How can I unlock human potential in the current circumstances?" and "What strategies can create resilient mindsets?" These questions triggered a surge of creative ideas on how I could contribute meaningfully during the pandemic. Driven by this newfound refreshment of my purpose, I embarked on a journey of reaching out to individuals, developing an online course on resilience, sharing insights on social media, and collaborating with various organisations. The realisation again that I had a purpose beyond myself became the driving force behind my inspiration and motivation. It propelled me to connect with diverse individuals, offering them tools to navigate the challenges posed by the pandemic. From conducting online sessions to facilitating discussions with teams worldwide on platforms like Zoom, I was fuelled by the belief that developing resilience and a thriving mindset was not only possible but imperative during these trying times. In essence, my rediscovered purpose became a catalyst for action, transforming adversity into an opportunity for growth and contribution. It exemplifies the power of a higher calling—one that transcends personal setbacks and encourages us to offer something meaningful to the world.

Secondly, a sense of purpose provides a crucial sense of direction, especially during times of uncertainty. Knowing one's purpose acts as a guiding compass, helping you maintain focus and make decisions aligned with your values and goals. With the understanding that my purpose was to "unlock human potential," I approached each day with a singular intention: "How can I unlock human potential today?" This intentional mindset not only uncovered new opportunities but also enabled me to discern meaningful actions that resonated with my overarching purpose. Furthermore, a well-defined purpose creates a positive mindset, allowing you to view challenges as opportunities for growth and learning. Those with a clear sense of purpose are inclined to approach adversity with optimism, recognising the potential for personal and professional development. Picture the visionary CEO who, fuelled by a mission to revolutionise their industry, views market disruptions as chances to innovate, adapt, and shape a more sustainable future for their company and its stakeholders.

Lastly, the process of identifying and embracing one's purpose enhances self-awareness through introspection. This self-discovery journey empowers individuals to understand their strengths, values, and priorities. Armed with this self-awareness, individuals are better equipped to build resilience by aligning their actions with their core beliefs. In essence, a clearly defined sense of purpose not only acts as a motivator but also as a compass, a source of optimism, and a catalyst for self-awareness, contributing to the growth of personal resilience in diverse aspects of life.

Now that we have explored the significance of recognising our purpose in cultivating resilience, the question arises: how do we go about discovering our why? This is a dynamic process with multiple pathways, and it's important to recognise that understanding our purpose is an ongoing journey throughout our lives. While gaining clarity on our why is important, it's equally vital not to become overly fixated on achieving 100% certainty in this exploration. There exist numerous approaches to unravelling our purpose, each offering unique insights into our values, passions, and strengths. The process involves self-reflection, exploration, and a willingness to experiment with different activities that align with our values and aspirations. While the quest for understanding our purpose may not lead to instant and absolute clarity, the journey itself holds immense value. It's about cultivating a continuous awareness of our evolving Why, allowing it to shape and redefine itself as we navigate the various chapters of our lives. Embracing the fluidity of this process not only enhances our resilience but also opens the door to a more authentic and purpose-driven existence.

The revelation of my purpose unfolded later in life, even though I had been instinctively fulfilling various facets of it, often more subconsciously than consciously. The crystallisation of this purpose occurred through introspection, as I dedicated time to reflect on elements of my life that brought me joy and fulfilment. However, the true clarity emerged when I reflected on my 20-year career in sales. While I found satisfaction in crafting sales strategies and propelling companies toward new growth horizons, a significant realisation dawned upon me. In hindsight, the moments when I felt truly in my element, effortlessly immersed in my work, were those instances where I was actively contributing to the development of someone in my team. Identifying and nurturing the latent talent within my team members became a source of profound fulfilment. This aspect of my role resonated so deeply with me that I took the initiative to create a competency model—a strategic tool designed to identify and cultivate the unique strengths of each team member. A competency model is a formal framework used in performance appraisals that outlines the particular abilities, traits, and behaviours needed to carry out a role effectively. Based on this, employee performance is assessed, areas of strength and improvement are noted, and professional development is directed. The development of this model stemmed from my genuine passion for helping others unlock their potential, signifying a turning point in my journey toward aligning my professional endeavours with my true purpose.

As with myself, embarking on a journey to discover your why or purpose involves a thoughtful exploration of your values, passions, strengths, life experiences, and aspirations. Firstly, reflect on your values and passions by contemplating the activities and subjects that you are passionate about. For instance, if building relationships and being of service to others is in line with your values, your purpose might revolve around community building or mentorship. Identifying your strengths is equally important in uncovering your purpose. Consider the skills that come effortlessly to you and the areas where you excel. If effective communication is one of your strengths, this may lead you to a purpose centred around inspiring and influencing others, perhaps through public speaking or writing. Examine your life experiences, particularly those that have been transformative. Personal examples could include overcoming a significant challenge, navigating a life-changing decision, or experiencing a profound moment of clarity. These experiences often hold the seeds of your purpose, offering valuable insights into the impact you wish to have on the world.

Furthermore, contemplate what you want to contribute to the world. Reflect on issues or causes that evoke a sense of purpose within you. For instance, if environmental sustainability is a cause that you feel strongly about, your purpose might involve advocating for eco-friendly practices or contributing to conservation efforts. As you explore, don't shy away from experimentation. Engage in different activities or pursuits aligned with your values, passions, and strengths. Personal examples could include volunteering for a cause you're passionate about, taking up a hobby that brings you joy, or exploring a career path that aligns with your aspirations. Through these personal experiments, you'll gain firsthand insights into what truly resonates with you, refining your understanding of your unique purpose. Ultimately, view this journey of self-discovery as a dynamic process. Allow your evolving insights, shaped by personal examples and experiences, to guide you toward a purpose that authentically reflects who you are and what you aspire to contribute to the world.

Daily habits for resilience

Establishing daily habits is crucial for constructing a resilient foundation of emotional, physical, and psychological strength. This framework becomes instrumental in fortifying you to face life's unexpected challenges. For instance, I experienced the impact of such habits during a particularly distressing time when my daughter, over 4,000 miles away in Canada, had an accident that affected her spine, potentially leading to paralysis – fortunately, she was fine. This unforeseen and emotionally charged situation left me grappling with feelings of helplessness and anxiety. The inability to be physically present compounded the stress, highlighting the significance of a robust daily routine to navigate through such challenging times. These real-life scenarios are a testament to the unpredictable nature of life, where unforeseen events can threaten to derail us. However, by diligently adhering to daily habits that promote emotional well-being and resilience, we equip ourselves to confront these challenges without completely unravelling. While the initial shock may disrupt our composure, the consistent practice of these habits ensures a return to a place of calmness, creating the resilience needed to navigate through life's unexpected twists and turns. I incorporate four essential habits into my daily routine: expressing gratitude, celebrating successes, engaging in reflection, and practising mindfulness.

Gratitude

Gratitude, as defined by Robert Emmons, a prominent psychology professor at the University of California, comprises two integral aspects. Firstly, it involves an acknowledgement of goodness, urging individuals to awaken to the positive aspects surrounding them and recognise the gifts they've received. Secondly, gratitude extends beyond oneself, emphasising the realisation that the source of this goodness originates externally—from other people, higher powers, fate, or the natural world. In essence, gratitude serves as a reminder that individuals owe their current position and blessings to the contributions of others. Psychologists Shai Davidai and Thomas Gilovich draw attention to a cognitive bias called the "Headwinds/Tailwinds Asymmetry," which implies that people tend to focus on life's problems and difficulties since solving them requires action. On the other hand, favourable features could go overlooked since they are thought to be inherent and low maintenance. Gilovich promotes the practice of gratefulness as a potent way to redirect attention toward the things that are good and give us the strength to move forward in life.

Studies have demonstrated that expressing appreciation on a daily basis releases feel-good neurotransmitters like serotonin and dopamine (Korb, 2012). According to scientific studies, gratefulness is essential for emotional resilience because it helps people focus on the positive elements of life, fight negative thought patterns, and develop a solution-focused mentality. It promotes maintaining present-moment awareness in the face of adversity and helps develop emotional resilience (Emmons and McCullough, 2003). The advantages of gratefulness practices become clear when one considers the cross-sectional study published in the International Journal of Social Psychiatry (Iqbal and Dar, 2018). This study found a strong positive link between resilience, happiness, and gratitude. The study, which included a large sample of adults, showed that people who practiced gratitude—especially by keeping a journal—reported happier and more resilient emotions. A follow-up study on patients with depression also revealed that those who participated in gratitude exercises recovered more quickly and were more driven to help themselves along the journey towards mental wellness (Gierveld, Dykstra and Schenk, 2012).

In conclusion, gratefulness manifests as a transforming energy that promotes emotional stability and resilience while refocusing attention on the good. Maintain a gratitude diary to help you incorporate gratefulness into your everyday activities. Write down three things for which you are grateful every day. They can be as simple as a lovely sunset or a kind word from a friend. You should think about giving someone who has improved your day a vocal thank you. Engage in mindful gratitude practices during moments of stress to shift your focus to positive aspects.

Celebrate success

Another critical habit is celebrating success, both on a personal and team level. Regularly acknowledging and celebrating achievements, no matter how small, contributes to a positive state of mind and maintains a future-focused perspective. This habit ensures that you recognise progress and milestones, reinforcing a mindset that propels you forward on your journey. In the rhythm of my daily life, whether I've successfully onboarded a new client, achieved noteworthy milestones with my podcast, or facilitated an impactful session with a client, I try to pause and celebrate these accomplishments. The celebrations take various forms; sometimes, it's a casual sharing of the achievement with my wife, a moment to express gratitude and joy. Other times, a small but meaningful gesture involves raising a toast with a glass of wine, savouring the moment in quiet reflection. For more significant achievements, the celebration might extend to a special meal, where the success can be embraced and commemorated more elaborately. The key principle remains consistent – it's not about the grandiosity of the achievement or the scale of the celebration; rather, it's about the intentional act of recognition. Taking the time to acknowledge these moments, big or small, cultivates a mindset of gratitude and reflection, reinforcing the significance of each step forward.

Celebrating accomplishments, no matter how minor, becomes a practice of mindfulness, instilling a positive and appreciative approach to both personal and professional victories. I would encourage you to celebrate both personal and team successes regularly. Create a system of acknowledging achievements, whether big or small. This could involve setting weekly goals and celebrating when they are met. Acknowledge the contributions of your colleagues by openly appreciating and encouraging their efforts. Celebrating success creates an uplifting and motivating atmosphere, propelling you and your team towards achieving future goals.

Reflection

Reflection stands as an important yet often underestimated tool in fortifying emotional resilience. Allocating time for thoughtful contemplation, whether in professional or personal realms, encourages a profound processing of experiences, leading to heightened self-awareness and a more mindful approach to life. This practice extends beyond surface-level thought, exploring the depths of the subconscious to unveil insights into both situations and emotions. The outcomes of reflective practices encompass new learning, fresh perspectives, and an augmented understanding of oneself—all important elements contributing to emotional resilience. Establishing a daily routine for dedicated reflection is crucial, and identifying the optimal setting varies from person to person; for someone like me, it may be whilst in nature while walking or running; while for others, it could be in the solitude of a comfortable chair. The process of reflection involves deliberate introspection, where you set aside time in a quiet space to ponder your experiences, thoughts, and actions. By posing open-ended questions and maintaining a reflective journal, you can gain profound insights into your emotions and reactions. Here are some questions you could ask yourself:

What is one thing I learned about myself today?

In what ways did I step out of my comfort zone or grow as an individual?

What was the most significant challenge I faced today?

How did I approach and navigate this challenge, and what did I learn from it?

How did I prioritise my well-being today?

What activities or practices brought me a sense of calm or joy?

Acknowledging achievements and learning from challenges become integral components of this reflective journey, guiding yourself to celebrate successes and perceive setbacks as avenues for growth. Setting improvement goals based on these reflections enables the creation of actionable steps for ongoing personal and professional development. Reflection, a dynamic and evolving practice, benefits from experimentation with different methods, ensuring a personalised approach aligned with individual preferences. Regular review and adjustment of reflections contribute to an unceasing journey of self-discovery and improvement. Thus, carving out a quiet space to contemplate experiences, positive and challenging alike, and adopting journaling as a tool for processing thoughts and emotions stand as effective means to enhance resilience. Consistently revisiting these reflections unveils behavioural patterns and areas ripe for personal growth.

Mindfulness

Mindfulness, which is another word for "presence," means focusing on the present moment without judging it. For this practice to work, you need to pay attention to your surroundings, your thoughts, your feelings, and how your body feels. The aim is to nurture heightened awareness of the present and promote clarity, focus, and a serene state. But how does this contribute to building personal resilience? Mindfulness contributes significantly to personal resilience by supporting emotional regulation and reducing stress. It achieves this by enhancing the brain's ability to process sensory information effectively.

Scientific research (Nakamura et al., 2021) suggests that engaging in mindfulness practices, such as meditation and deep breathing, positively influences the brain's cognitive processes. Specifically, mindfulness increases the weight of output from regions responsible for processing sensory stimuli from the external world, like the thalamus and sensory cortex. This heightened sensory information activates areas such as the insula and anterior cingulate cortex, which play important roles in emotional regulation. As a result, the orbitofrontal cortex and dorsolateral prefrontal cortex step in to inhibit the activity of the amygdala—a key centre for emotions. This process is akin to top-down emotion regulation, where the brain consciously controls emotional responses. In simpler terms, mindfulness helps individuals navigate challenges by improving the brain's ability to process and regulate emotions. By incorporating mindfulness into daily routines, individuals can develop a more resilient mindset, better equipped to face life's inevitable ups and downs.

One personal example of mindfulness that I incorporate into my daily routine is box breathing. This structured breathing exercise involves inhaling for four counts, holding the breath for four counts, exhaling for four counts, and then maintaining an empty breath for another four counts. This intentional and rhythmic breathing pattern not only enhances my mindfulness practice but also provides a tangible framework for managing stress and promoting a sense of calm and focus. Box breathing serves as a powerful tool for maintaining a heightened awareness of the present moment and building personal resilience in the face of daily challenges. Moreover, while the essence of mindfulness lies in being present in the moment, I encourage my clients to explore various techniques that resonate with them. These techniques can range from practicing yoga or meditation to engaging in activities that allow them to fully immerse themselves in the present. One effective approach is to guide clients in recalling a specific instance when they experienced a profound sense of presence and then incorporate elements of that experience into their daily lives. For some individuals, playing a musical instrument serves as a powerful tool for achieving mindfulness, as it demands complete focus and attention. Others may find solace in embarking on a solitary walk in nature, taking the time to consciously observe and appreciate the surrounding sights, sounds, and sensations. The key is to discover and cultivate personal methods of practicing mindfulness that align with your unique preferences and lifestyle.

Cold water

A consistent practice that I have maintained for the past two and a half years involves daily immersion in cold water, either in an ice bath in my garden, a cold shower, or weekends spent in the sea with friends. This deliberate engagement in cold water induces a range of physiological responses designed to adapt to the challenging environment. Initial vasoconstriction and narrowing of blood vessels, redirects blood flow away from extremities, elevating heart rate and blood pressure. Simultaneously, this triggers the release of stress hormones like adrenaline and cortisol, reminiscent of the ingrained "fight or flight" response in our evolutionary biology. Additionally, there's a substantial 3 to 4-fold increase in dopamine over 2-3 hours (Srámek et al., 2000), creating a positive "high" sensation and increased mental focus and clarity. By integrating this daily cold-water immersion into my routine, I have personally witnessed its transformative impact on resilience.

Engaging in regular cold-water immersion has led to a remarkable increase in my ability to handle stress. I've observed that it now requires a more significant level of stress to affect me noticeably. The immediate aftermath of each invigorating ice bath brings about a heightened sense of focus and mental clarity, creating a refreshing mental state. Notably, my previous anxiety associated with networking has entirely dissipated. In situations where anxiety is a common response, particularly before networking events, I now find myself unaffected by stress. It's not just a matter of familiarity; rather, these situations seem to have lost their ability to register as stressful experiences for me. This transformation speaks to the profound impact of cold-water immersion on not only stress resilience but also cognitive functioning and social anxiety.

This routine exposure to discomfort serves as a powerful

mechanism for cultivating tolerance to stress, both physically and mentally. Much like strengthening a muscle through consistent exercise, the repeated activation of the stress response over time equips you to navigate the challenges of daily life with heightened fortitude. Beyond the immediate physiological effects, the practice of cold-water immersion also becomes a training ground for emotional regulation and stress management. Learning to endure and adapt to the discomfort associated with cold exposure translates into an improved ability to regulate emotions and control reactions to various stressors. This heightened emotional resilience, honed through regular cold water immersion, extends its benefits beyond the specific practice, enabling you to face challenging situations in your daily lives with greater composure and adaptive capacity. In essence, deliberate exposure to cold water serves as a dynamic tool for developing both physical and emotional resilience. By integrating this practice into my daily routine, I witness the tangible effects on my ability to confront discomfort, manage stress, and cultivate enduring resilience in the face of life's inevitable challenges.

Incorporating these habits into daily life not only promotes emotional resilience but also contributes to overall well-being. They serve as powerful tools in navigating life's challenges, creating a positive mindset, and cultivating the internal strength needed for sustained growth and thriving.

Creating a supportive community

Building personal resilience is a dynamic process that extends beyond individual efforts, with the community playing an important role in strengthening one's ability to navigate life's challenges. At its core, a supportive community around you acts as a vital safety net, offering emotional sustenance during trying times. The presence of individuals who genuinely care about your well-being provides a foundation for emotional support, helping to alleviate stress and anxiety. Knowing that you are not alone in facing difficulties, and having a network that empathises with your experiences, enhances your emotional resilience.

Reflecting on the early days of our journey into becoming foster carers stirs a myriad of emotions. Despite the thorough training and preparations my wife and I underwent, the experience proved to be a significant challenge. The child we welcomed into our home had endured trauma and upheaval, moving through multiple foster homes before arriving at our home. This transition was undoubtedly a huge shock for her, and navigating the complexities of fostering became an emotional test for our family. Amid these trials, the support of our close-knit friends became indispensable. Their understanding of the complex path we had travelled to become foster carers, coupled with their steadfast physical and emotional assistance, became invaluable. In moments when the weight of our responsibilities seemed overwhelming, our friends were there for us. They provided not only a listening ear but also a safe space to share the challenges we encountered. This robust support network played an important role in ensuring the successful placement of our foster daughter. Now, over five years later, she has seamlessly woven herself into the fabric of our family. The journey was undoubtedly both challenging and rewarding, but the unwavering support of our friends remains a testament to the resilience and strength that can be found in shared experiences and genuine connections.

Furthermore, the profound sense of belonging, cultivated within a community, is key in developing individual resilience. This sentiment of connection to a collective of individuals who resonate with shared values, experiences, or aspirations serves as a dynamic catalyst for enhancing one's sense of purpose and identity. This shared belonging is not only a testament to unity but also operates as a protective shield, establishing a robust support system that significantly strengthens mental and emotional well-being, especially in the face of adversity. Consider, for instance, a close-knit neighbourhood where residents actively engage in communal events and shared responsibilities. The bonds formed through these communal activities create a network of support during challenging times, such as the aftermath of a natural disaster or a personal crisis. The shared sense of belonging in this community not only ensures that individuals feel cared for but also fosters a collaborative spirit, enabling them to weather challenges collectively.

In professional spheres, being part of a workplace community can significantly impact individual resilience. A team that shares a common vision and values, where employees feel connected to a greater purpose, establishes a supportive ecosystem. During demanding projects or periods of uncertainty, this shared sense of belonging supports a culture of collaboration, encouraging team members to pool their strengths and navigate challenges together. Moreover, the protective influence of community belonging is evident in groups like support networks for individuals facing health challenges. Whether it's a cancer support group or an online community for mental health, the shared experiences and understanding within these communities create an environment where individuals find solace and strength in each other. This shared sense of belonging becomes a vital source of emotional support, aiding in the resilience of each member facing their unique struggles. In essence, the sense of belonging within a community goes beyond mere connection; it acts as a transformative force that bolsters individual resilience. By creating a shared purpose, identity, and support system, communities become powerful allies in navigating life's challenges, enriching the collective resilience of their members.

The communities and networks that surround us play a crucial role, serving not only as pillars of support but also as invaluable platforms for nurturing resilience skills through exposure to diverse perspectives. This became evident to me a few years ago when my business faced considerable challenges, subsequently impacting me on a personal level as I endeavoured to steer the business back to success. The significance of having individuals in your circle with whom you can share challenges, and who offer their advice and diverse perspectives, cannot be overstated. During the trying times of my struggling business, a suggestion emerged to connect with another business owner in a similar field who was actively seeking associates. This idea had not crossed my mind previously, and it presented an opportunity not only to secure new work but also to acquire fresh knowledge and expand my support network. This turned out to be a transformative solution to my challenges, bringing in not just new projects but also broadening my mindset. Consequently, various aspects of my business began to unfold in unexpected ways. This experience underscored the power of engaging with others possessing different perspectives, proving that collaboration and shared insights can be instrumental in overcoming challenges and fostering personal and professional growth.

Interacting with individuals who bring varied life experiences to the communal table becomes a rich source of learning and growth. Engaging with such diversity presents opportunities to explore alternative ways of coping and problem-solving, thus contributing significantly to the development of a robust set of resilience skills. Consider a community initiative that brings together individuals from different cultural backgrounds to collaborate on a shared project. The diversity within this group exposes participants to a wealth of perspectives on navigating challenges. Through the exchange of ideas and approaches, individuals learn to adapt their problem-solving strategies, drawing inspiration from the varied experiences and cultural insights within the community.

In professional settings, being part of a diverse workplace community provides a similar opportunity for skill enrichment. Teams comprising individuals with diverse skills, backgrounds, and perspectives are better equipped to confront complex challenges. The collaborative synergy that arises creates an environment where each member contributes unique problem-solving approaches. For instance, a team working on a global project may benefit from the diverse perspectives of its members, incorporating a range of cultural insights into their strategies for overcoming obstacles. Moreover, the learning process within a community extends beyond theoretical knowledge to practical insights gained from shared experiences.

In a community that embraces resilience as a collective goal, individuals often share personal stories of facing and overcoming challenges. For example, a community support group for individuals dealing with job loss may provide a platform for members to share their experiences and the strategies that helped them navigate career transitions successfully. This exchange not only imparts practical wisdom but also encourages a culture of collective growth and empowerment. In essence, communities serve as dynamic ecosystems where diverse perspectives converge to enrich individuals' resilience toolkits. The exposure to alternative coping mechanisms, the amalgamation of various problem-solving approaches, and the shared experiences of overcoming challenges create a culture of continuous learning and collective empowerment within the community.

In moments of crisis, the true strength of a community manifests as they unite in a concerted effort to deliver swift and organised support. Whether faced with the aftermath of a natural disaster or navigating through personal tragedy, a community's capacity to come together becomes a cornerstone for effective response. This collective mobilisation not only addresses immediate needs but also serves as a powerful testament to the interconnectedness and resilience inherent in the fabric of the community. Consider a community rallying together after a devastating flood. Residents, local businesses, and organisations work together to provide emergency relief, shelter, and assistance to those affected. This collective response not only ensures the rapid provision of essentials but also establishes a network of support that extends beyond the crisis. The shared effort reinforces the notion that, in times of adversity, a unified community can be a formidable force for recovery and renewal. In a more personal context, communities often demonstrate remarkable cohesion when faced with individual tragedies. A tightly knit neighbourhood, for example, may come together to support a family dealing with a sudden loss. From organising meals to offering emotional comfort, this communal response becomes a lifeline for those undergoing challenging times. The strength of the community lies not just in addressing immediate needs but in creating an enduring sense of solidarity and care. Essentially, the cultivation of personal resilience intertwines with the fostering and maintenance of community ties.

I encourage you to evaluate the community around you and take proactive steps to construct a strong support network. Establishing a robust and supportive community requires deliberate actions to develop authentic connections. Whether in personal or professional spheres, actively engaging with others, participating in relevant events or groups, and demonstrating authenticity are fundamental. Networking events, social gatherings, and online platforms offer opportunities to connect with like-minded individuals. Genuine relationships flourish when built on shared interests, transparent communication, and a readiness to provide support. Dedicate time to understanding others, extend assistance when possible, and embrace diverse perspectives to contribute to the development of a resilient and mutually beneficial community. Ultimately, building a community involves seeking connections, nurturing relationships, and actively contributing to the well-being of those within your community.

Chapter summary

The chapter on personal resilience complements the discussion on team resilience by emphasising the interconnectedness of individual well-being and overall team effectiveness. It presents a three-point strategy for cultivating personal resilience: (1) clarity of purpose, which serves as a guiding light and motivator; (2) daily habits for resilience, including gratitude, celebrating successes, reflection, mindfulness, and exposure to discomfort through cold water immersion; and (3) building a supportive community that provides emotional sustenance, a sense of belonging, diverse perspectives, collective strength, and a platform for nurturing resilience skills. The chapter underscores the importance of developing personal resilience as a holistic contributor to a resilient team, offering practical insights, actionable strategies, and thoughtful reflections to empower individuals in navigating life's challenges.

Reflection

What does having a clearly defined sense of purpose mean to you, and how has it influenced your life so far?

Can you recall a challenging time in your life when revisiting your purpose or "why" provided motivation and inspiration?

Consider the impact of daily gratitude journaling on your well-being. How has consciously acknowledging positive aspects shifted your focus and mindset?

Explore the outcomes of regular reflection in your life. How has thoughtful contemplation led to new learning, fresh perspectives, and an enhanced understanding of yourself?

Recall a challenging time in your life and reflect on how the support of your community or network impacted your resilience.

Explore ways to strengthen your existing communities or build new connections to enhance your resilience.

Action

Take time to identify and articulate your core values. What principles guide your decision-making and actions?

Craft a vision board that visually represents your goals and aspirations. What images, quotes, or symbols resonate with your sense of purpose?

Dedicate time for daily reflection, experimenting with different methods to understand your emotions and experiences better.

To improve emotional regulation, incorporate mindfulness exercises into your routine, such as meditation or deep breathing.

Actively participate in community events and shared responsibilities. How can you contribute to building a sense of community in your surroundings?

Encourage a positive work environment. How can you support an environment at work that encourages cooperation and shared goals?

CHAPTER FOUR:
CREATING PSYCHOLOGICAL SAFETY

What you will gain from this chapter

A deep understanding of how psychological safety is crucial for building resilient teams.

Insights into the impact of interpersonal risk on team dynamics and performance.

Real-life examples and personal narratives that illustrate the transformative power of psychological safety in creating innovation, collaboration, and adaptability.

Practical strategies for cultivating a psychologically safe environment within your team, promoting open communication, risk-taking, and learning from mistakes.

Insight: The environment is key

Have you ever had the feeling that venturing a risk within your team or organisation could lead to repercussions if things don't unfold as planned? Or maybe you've noticed shortcomings in certain leadership strategies but hesitated to voice your perspective. This recurring scenario has been a common theme in some organisations I've experienced, encapsulating the essence of a psychologically unsafe workplace. In such an environment, open communication is actively discouraged, and leadership assumes an authoritarian posture, instilling a pervasive fear among employees. The absence of acknowledgement and support cultivates sentiments of undervaluation and demotivation. Unaddressed bullying, harassment, and unfair policies contribute to a culture of mistrust, resulting in high turnover of staff, low morale, and limited growth opportunities that leave individuals feeling constrained and frustrated. The enduring emotional strain of stress and anxiety infiltrates the workplace, creating an unhealthy atmosphere that undermines both individual well-being and the organisation's success.

Jona Wright, EdD, Founder and Principal Consultant, Jona Wright, LLC, shared that when discussing psychological safety, openness in communication and a willingness to take risks is crucial for building resilient teams. Jona suggests that in an environment where talent is consistently undermined or injured, true resilience may be lacking, possibly leading individuals to disengage or give up as a form of coping. The reason that I highlight psychologically unsafe teams is that, in contrast, a psychologically safe team helps create an environment where members feel secure expressing themselves, taking risks, and being vulnerable. This, in turn, cultivates resilience, enabling teams to thrive long-term, adapt continuously, rebound from setbacks, and stand united in the face of challenges.

During my career, I have encountered workplaces where the lack of psychological safety created a situation where challenging leadership was a daunting prospect. The organisational hierarchy had created an environment where questioning decisions or proposing alternative approaches was viewed with scepticism rather than curiosity. As I navigated my role, there were instances where I observed decisions that seemed counterintuitive or potentially detrimental to our objectives. However, the prevailing culture made it clear that challenging these decisions could be perceived as insubordination. The fear of backlash or being labelled as a dissenting voice stifled any inclination to express concerns about leadership choices. The leadership style was authoritative, and dissenting opinions were not welcomed. This created a dynamic where employees, including myself, felt compelled to conform rather than voice legitimate concerns. The absence of open dialogue with leadership hindered the organisation's ability to leverage the diverse perspectives within the team. The absence of psychological safety in challenging leadership decisions created a culture of conformity. It became increasingly evident that a workplace where leaders were resistant to constructive criticism or diverse viewpoints was not conducive to my growth and professional fulfilment. This challenging dynamic with leadership, where openness and dialogue were discouraged, played a significant role in my decision to seek a more inclusive and psychologically safe work environment. The experience highlighted the importance of leadership that encourages open communication, values diverse perspectives, and encourages employees to challenge decisions constructively for the benefit of the organisation.

Reflecting on my own negative experience in a corporate setting, it becomes apparent that the presence of psychological safety is crucial for a thriving and innovative workplace. Contrasting this with the success stories of organisations like Pixar Animation Studios sheds light on an important distinction. High-performing teams, like those at Pixar, thrive on psychological safety—an element absent in environments that hinder performance. In my experience, the lack of this crucial component stifled creativity and innovation. The leadership's intolerance towards risks and aversion to open dialogue meant that mistakes were met with punishment rather than viewed as opportunities for growth. Ed Catmull, President of Pixar, once reflected that "Candor couldn't happen without trust, and trust required an environment in which risks weren't punished." The observation made at Pixar resonates with my own experience, emphasising the critical role of psychological safety. In stark contrast, examining Unilever's commitment to psychological safety underscores its transformative impact. Unilever, unlike my own experience, actively supports an inclusive culture where diverse perspectives are not only encouraged but celebrated. The company acknowledges that true innovation emerges from a rich blend of ideas and perspectives. By championing psychological safety, Unilever empowers its workforce to express ideas openly, challenge norms, and contribute fearlessly. The outcomes are not merely products on the market; they signify the strength that emerges when individuals feel secure enough to explore, experiment, and contribute their unique talents. The stark contrast between these experiences, coupled with insights from Pixar, highlights the transformative power of psychological safety in shaping resilient, innovative, and collaborative work cultures.

What is psychological safety?

What is psychological safety precisely, and how does it support resilience? I describe it as a setting where individuals feel free to speak up, show vulnerability, and take chances without worrying about shame, reprisals, or punishment. It is marked by interpersonal trust and mutual respect. After being studied for the first time by early organisational scholars in the 1960s, psychological safety research was neglected for a while until gaining traction again in the 1990s, and continues to this day. In light of the increased emphasis on learning and innovation in modern companies, I suggest that the renewed interest in psychological safety is related to its expanding theoretical and practical value.

The increasing prominence of psychological safety in organisational discourse can be largely attributed to its critical role in mitigating interpersonal risk. Interpersonal risk refers to the potential consequences that may emerge from engaging in social interactions or relationships with others. It encompasses the vulnerability and uncertainty individuals face when opening up, sharing personal information, or expressing opinions and ideas in a social setting. In the context of organisations, interpersonal risk can manifest in various forms, such as the fear of being rejected, embarrassed, or facing conflicts with colleagues or line managers. These apprehensions can hinder open communication, stifle creativity, and impede collaboration, ultimately undermining individual and team performance.

Psychological safety is how individuals perceive the potential outcomes of taking interpersonal risks in their work environment. It encompasses ingrained beliefs concerning others' likely responses when an individual exposes themselves, such as asking questions, seeking feedback, reporting errors, or suggesting new ideas. At critical decision points, individuals engage in an implicit evaluation, weighing the interpersonal risk associated with a specific action against the prevailing interpersonal atmosphere. In this assessment, "If I undertake X in this context, will I face harm, embarrassment, or criticism?" A negative response indicates the presence of psychological safety, enabling the individual to proceed. Consequently, an action that might be deemed unthinkable in one workplace could be embraced in another due to differing beliefs about the probable interpersonal consequences.

One notable example of demonstrating psychological safety is Google's Project Aristotle, which aimed to identify the key factors contributing to effective team performance. The study found that psychological safety was the most critical element for high-performing teams. In teams where members felt comfortable taking risks, admitting mistakes, and being vulnerable, innovation thrived. This insight led Google to emphasise the importance of developing psychological safety across its teams. Beyond Google's Project Aristotle, numerous organisations have recognised the important role of psychological safety in cultivating a work environment that encourages innovation, collaboration, and overall team effectiveness. Take the multinational corporation Procter & Gamble (P&G), for instance. P&G places a strong emphasis on fostering a culture where employees feel psychologically safe to express their ideas and opinions. This approach has been instrumental in driving creativity and problem-solving within project teams. Team members at P&G are encouraged to share diverse viewpoints, knowing that their input is valued and contributes to the collective success of the team.

Speaking from personal experience, I have seen firsthand in one of my valued clients, how important psychological safety is in a small business setting. In a small team setting, where everyone's input was valued, creating an atmosphere of trust and openness on purpose led to big changes. The friendly environment gave everyone on the team the courage to share their thoughts freely, come up with new ideas for how to solve problems, and learn from each other's shared experiences. The main thing that made this work was that mistakes weren't punished, which led to an attitude of trying new things and being flexible. This attitude of trying new things and being flexible, which was based on psychological safety, became a key part of the company's huge success. By getting rid of the fear of what might happen, team members felt free to take calculated risks, try new methods, and quickly change direction when needed. This created a company that not only dealt with problems effectively but also grew thanks to a foundation of trust and shared creativity. This personal experience shows how important and long-lasting feeling safe can be in the close quarters of a small business. Creating an open and trusting environment is more than just a good idea for the workplace; it's what makes the company successful, brings out the best in people, and helps the team reach its full potential.

These examples collectively illustrate that psychological safety is not limited to specific industries but is a universal factor that underpins effective teamwork and organisational success across diverse sectors. The recognition of its importance continues to grow, with more companies understanding that creating a psychologically safe workplace is a strategic imperative for fostering resilience, innovation, and sustained success. Research by Harvard Business School professor Amy Edmondson found that psychologically safe teams have more open and honest communication, are quicker to detect and prevent problems, and view failures as learning opportunities rather than occasions for blame or accusations. Rather than try to avoid criticism, team members admit weaknesses and mistakes, pool their insights, have lively debates about ideas without egos getting in the way, give and receive frequent feedback from each other, and approach issues from a shared mindset that "we are in this together."

What about trust?

While there are certain similarities between psychological safety and trust, it's essential to recognise their conceptual distinctions. Psychological safety primarily revolves around the perceptions of group members regarding a shared group norm. It delves into the collective understanding of how individuals within a group anticipate the consequences of taking interpersonal risks, creating an environment where members feel free to express ideas, seek feedback, or propose innovative solutions without fear of negative repercussions. On the other hand, trust operates on an individual level, emphasising how one person perceives another. It's about the confidence and reliance that an individual places on another's intentions, competence, and reliability. Trust is a foundational element in interpersonal relationships, focusing on the expectations and beliefs that one person holds about the character and behaviour of another. In essence, while psychological safety centres on the group dynamics and the perceived consequences of shared norms, trust is more personalised, dealing with individual assessments of reliability and credibility in interpersonal interactions. Both are crucial aspects of healthy organisational relationships, contributing to a collaborative and supportive work environment.

Reminder of resilience in the context of psychological safety

At the core of resilience lies the capacity to not only persist and push through setbacks and challenges but, more importantly, to glean valuable lessons from these experiences. Resilience is not just about endurance; it's about navigating difficulties with a strategic mindset. In the context of a team, fostering resilience involves a shift in thinking, the generation of innovative ideas, and the creation of novel approaches. Crucial to this process is the active participation of team members, who must feel empowered to voice their opinions openly. In the pursuit of resilience, teams often embark on uncharted territories, employing strategies and approaches that might be entirely new to them. This inherent novelty introduces an element of risk, as these untested methods may not yield the desired outcomes. However, it is precisely through this risk-taking that teams can uncover innovative solutions and embrace the potential for growth. The willingness to experiment with new ways of thinking and working is a fundamental aspect of team resilience, providing the foundation for sustained success.

Suzie Lewis, MD at Transform for Value, shares that fostering resilience, psychological safety, openness, and trust is essential.

Suzie emphasises the importance of embracing failure, seeing it as an opportunity to pivot and adapt. Recalling instances where budget cuts could have been catastrophic, the team demonstrated a collective mindset to navigate challenges. The dynamic involved team members, including unexpected leaders, stepping up to encourage innovative thinking and collaboration. This experience highlighted the significance of shared responsibility and a willingness to think differently, developing resilience in the face of adversity. In the context of open communication, team members were empowered to voice their opinions and contribute to discussions, creating a rich exchange of perspectives. This exchange not only leads to a deeper understanding of various viewpoints but also enhances the team's adaptability and resilience in the face of challenges. By establishing an environment where individuals feel heard and valued, open communication becomes a catalyst for building a cohesive and resilient team, capable of collaboratively overcoming obstacles and achieving shared goals.

A prime example of the positive impact of psychological safety on innovation is evident in tech companies that encourage employees to propose new projects or ideas without the fear of punitive measures. Google's famous "20% time" policy is a noteworthy illustration, where employees are granted 20% of their work time to pursue personal projects of interest. This approach has yielded several innovative products, including Gmail and Google Maps. Furthermore, the willingness to embrace a culture of experimentation and innovation is integral to a team's adaptability in the face of dynamic circumstances. By cultivating an environment where calculated risks are not only tolerated but encouraged, teams become better equipped to navigate challenges and proactively respond to changing situations. This adaptability, fuelled by a spirit of innovation, is a key component of resilience, ensuring that teams can evolve and thrive even amid uncertainty and ambiguity.

Consider the aviation industry, where a culture of learning from mistakes is ingrained through systems like the Aviation Safety Reporting System (ASRS). Pilots, air traffic controllers, and other aviation professionals can confidentially report errors and near misses without the fear of retribution. This has led to a wealth of information on safety improvements, contributing to the continuous enhancement of aviation practices. One important part of building resilience in teams is learning from mistakes. It serves as a dynamic feedback loop, allowing for the constant refinement of strategies and approaches. In an environment where errors are acknowledged, analysed, and transformed into insights, teams can adapt and evolve, ultimately becoming more robust in the face of challenges.

An exemplary illustration of psychological safety facilitating adaptability is observed in companies that prioritise a culture of innovation, such as Amazon. The company encourages experimentation and the exploration of new business ideas, allowing teams to adapt swiftly to market changes and evolving customer preferences. This adaptability has played a crucial role in Amazon's ability to diversify its offerings and remain at the forefront of the e-commerce industry. The importance of adaptability and flexibility is magnified when considering resilience within a team. A resilient team possesses the capacity to seamlessly adapt to new circumstances and rebound resiliently from setbacks. Psychological safety acts as a catalyst in developing and nurturing this adaptability, ensuring that team members are not only willing but also enthusiastic about embracing change.

In an environment where team members feel secure in expressing their thoughts and ideas without fear of judgment, a natural inclination towards collaboration emerges. This trust and mutual support form the foundation of resilience, especially during challenging periods when cohesive teamwork becomes paramount. An example of psychological safety fostering collaboration can be seen in the healthcare sector, where interdisciplinary teams work together to deliver patient care. In such an environment, nurses, doctors, and various specialists collaborate, pooling their expertise to address complex medical cases. The trust and support within the team contribute not only to improved patient outcomes but also to the overall well-being and job satisfaction of the healthcare professionals involved. Collaborative efforts within psychologically safe teams extend beyond mere cooperation; they represent a synergy of strengths, resources, and diverse perspectives. This pooling of collective capabilities enhances the team's overall ability to confront and surmount obstacles effectively. By combining individual talents and insights, the team becomes more adaptable and resilient, navigating challenges with a shared sense of purpose and a unified approach.

The widespread fear of failing can be effectively countered by creating a psychologically safe team environment. This frees team members from the worries that come with making mistakes. When people on a team are sure that their contributions won't get them in trouble, they are more likely to take calculated risks, explore uncharted territory, and try out new ways of doing things without constantly worrying about what might go wrong. An illuminating example of psychological safety mitigating the fear of failure is evident in the tech industry, particularly in companies renowned for innovation. For instance, Google is known for its "fail fast, fail often" attitude, which tells teams to try new things and learn from their mistakes early on in the development process. This way of working has not only produced ground-breaking products, but it has also made the workplace a place where failure is much less likely to happen.

Teams that don't have to worry about failing are better able to deal with problems because their members are more likely to think outside the box, take risks, and try different methods. This greater freedom to try new things and change with the times becomes a key part of making the team more resilient. Creating an environment where mistakes are seen as chances to learn and get better is one way that psychological safety helps a team recover from failures, accept change, and grow when things go wrong. When people don't fear failing as much, they can build stronger teams that can do well in settings that are always changing.

In summary, psychological safety is important in building team resilience because it creates an atmosphere conducive to open communication, risk-taking, learning from mistakes, adaptability, collaboration, reduced fear of failure, and shared responsibility. These factors collectively contribute to a team's ability to withstand challenges, adapt to change, and emerge stronger from setbacks.

An example of creating psychological safety in your team – the How

I have crafted an illustration demonstrating the establishment of a psychologically safe environment through a fictional case study. Drawing from both personal experiences and extensive studies on the subject, this example aims to provide practical insights into fostering psychological safety.

Case study

When Anne assumed the role of customer service manager at a food manufacturing company, she faced a disheartened and overwhelmed team. Customer complaints were on the rise, accompanied by a noticeable spike in response times. Recognising that a mere emphasis on technical training wouldn't suffice unless team members felt supported to devise creative solutions, Anne drew from best practices on psychological safety to transform the team's dynamics. To encourage openness and trust and increase the team's resilience, Anne implemented several key strategies:

Encouraging a no-blame environment: Anne went beyond just making verbal assurances about a no-blame environment; she actively implemented measures to ensure it. This included setting up confidential channels for team members to share concerns anonymously, guaranteeing that their identities would be protected. Additionally, Anne organised periodic workshops focused on building trust and addressing any lingering apprehensions within the team. By incorporating these tangible safeguards, Anne not only communicated trust but also demonstrated a commitment to creating a secure platform for open communication. Team members felt confident that their input wouldn't lead to negative consequences, allowing them to express concerns freely.

Modelling vulnerability: Anne's commitment to modelling vulnerability extended to sharing personal anecdotes of challenges she faced and how she navigated them. This approach humanised her leadership, making her more relatable to the team. In team meetings, she would often initiate discussions about personal and professional setbacks that she encountered, creating an environment where team members saw vulnerability as a strength rather than a weakness. Anne's openness created an atmosphere where team members felt comfortable sharing their challenges, ultimately contributing to a more empathetic and supportive work environment.

Continuous empowerment of team members: Anne's empowerment strategy wasn't a one-off initiative; it was an ongoing process. She facilitated workshops and training sessions that equipped team members with the necessary skills and knowledge to actively contribute to decision-making. Moreover, Anne established a mentorship program within the team, creating opportunities for less experienced members to learn from their more seasoned colleagues. This continuous empowerment contributed to a dynamic team that consistently sought innovative solutions. Anne's emphasis on ongoing education and mentorship demonstrated her commitment to encouraging individual growth and collective excellence.

Deeply embedded failing forward culture: To cultivate a failing-forward culture, Anne went beyond applauding individual experiments. She initiated team-wide sessions where members shared their failures and the lessons learned. These sessions were not just about celebrating success but also acknowledging setbacks as valuable learning experiences. By institutionalising this practice, Anne ensured that the entire team embraced a mindset where failure was an integral part of the journey toward improvement. Anne actively participated in these sessions, sharing her own experiences of failure and emphasising the collective nature of the learning process. This created a culture of transparency and resilience, where setbacks were viewed as stepping stones to future success.

Structured open dialogue: Anne's encouragement of open dialogue wasn't confined to weekly touchpoints. She facilitated cross-functional brainstorming sessions, encouraging diverse perspectives and creating a culture of collaboration. This structured open dialogue, beyond enhancing communication, facilitated the exchange of ideas, ultimately contributing to a more innovative and adaptable team.

Active listening as a leadership principle: Anne's active listening wasn't solely limited to team meetings. She implemented a "listening tour" strategy, where she regularly scheduled one-on-one sessions with team members to understand their perspectives, challenges, and aspirations. This personalised approach not only showcased Anne's commitment to individual growth but also allowed her to tailor leadership strategies to the unique needs of each team member. Anne actively engaged in these sessions, asking probing questions and demonstrating genuine interest in the personal and professional development of her team members. This personalised approach to leadership strengthened the bond between Anne and her team, creating a sense of trust and loyalty.

Holistic acknowledgment of concerns: Anne's acknowledgement of concerns wasn't confined to expressing gratitude; she established a task force dedicated to addressing systemic issues highlighted by the team. This cross-functional team, led by Anne, proactively worked to implement long-term solutions, demonstrating a commitment to not just treating surface-level symptoms but fundamentally transforming the team's operational landscape. Anne initiated a comprehensive feedback mechanism, allowing team members to provide ongoing insights into challenges and opportunities. This proactive approach ensured that concerns were not only acknowledged but also translated into tangible actions, creating a culture of continuous improvement and adaptability.

In summary, Anne's multifaceted approach to creating psychological safety within her team encompassed tangible actions, and a holistic commitment to creating an environment where every team member felt valued, heard, and empowered. Through these comprehensive strategies, Anne successfully transformed the team dynamics, supporting a culture of collaboration, innovation, and resilience. The enduring impact of Anne's leadership was reflected in the team's heightened morale, increased creativity, and enhanced ability to navigate challenges collectively.

In conclusion, Anne's strategic implementation of psychological safety not only transformed the disheartened and overwhelmed customer service team but also paved the way for a remarkable cultural shift. By creating an environment where team members felt secure in expressing their thoughts and ideas, Anne not only addressed the immediate challenges but also nurtured a spirit of collaboration and innovation. The team's journey from a blame-free environment to embracing vulnerability and actively participating in decision-making exemplifies the profound impact of psychological safety on team dynamics. As a result, the positive changes manifested not only in improved internal processes and streamlined workflows but also in a significant reduction in response times and customer complaints. Ultimately, the boost in morale and the building of a sense of solidarity stand as tangible outcomes of Anne's commitment to cultivating psychological safety within her team, showcasing its transformative power in enhancing overall team resilience and success.

More exercises to help create psychological safety with your team

To further create the principles of psychological safety, I often use a simple yet powerful exercise when working with teams. This exercise is best facilitated by the leader or, ideally, a coach or someone from outside the team.

To begin, set aside ample time for this exercise, as allowing sufficient time is key. Create a "hot seat" where each team member will take turns sitting and listening to the feedback their colleagues share about them. It's common for people to feel uncomfortable with this process, as we are not often accustomed to publicly hearing positive contributions about ourselves. The person in the "hot seat" should simply sit, listen, and reflect on what is being said about them. Each team member then takes turns sharing their thoughts, answering these three questions about the person in the "hot seat":

What do you value about this person's contribution to the team?

What specific contributions do they make to the team's success?

What are their unique strengths?

Encourage everyone to contribute, even if it means sharing multiple times, as one person's insights may spark additional thoughts from others. Once everyone has finished sharing, invite the person in the "hot seat" to reflect and share their own thoughts on what has been said. This exercise reveals a great deal about each team member, breaking down barriers and developing trust within the team. It also helps to build psychological safety by creating a space for open, positive communication and recognition of each individual's value. Implementing this exercise can be a powerful tool in cultivating a team environment where everyone feels safe, valued, and empowered to contribute their best work.

Another exercise I have used and adapted from Cary Bailey-Findley from the High Performance Culture is a facilitated discussion. As with the previous exercise, ensure you allocate sufficient time for the conversation. The discussion revolves around four key questions, and it's important to ensure that everyone has the opportunity to share their thoughts. Be mindful that some team members might need more time to reflect and share, while others will contribute more readily.

Question 1: What are the strengths that you bring to the team?

Discussing our positive attributes and strengths is generally easier than sharing our weaknesses and mistakes. This first question is designed to highlight the strengths that each team member brings to the table, helping to open up the conversation. Encourage participants to provide real-life examples as they share their answers. Generic statements like "I'm very reliable" do not effectively build psychological safety. Instead, team members should share specific examples from their work that demonstrate their reliability.

Question 2: Which of your strengths are the team not making the most of right now?

In addition to the strengths we believe we contribute to the team, we all possess untapped potential. While some of these strengths might not be directly applicable in the work context, others could be valuable but are currently underutilised. For example, someone who is a qualified coach in the team may find that their coaching skills could benefit the team, even if they are not currently being used.

Question 3: What is a recent mistake that you made but learned a great deal from?

Psychological safety is not only about being confident in your strengths and contributions; it also involves being comfortable sharing your weaknesses or things that might embarrass you. To build this comfort, the team must shift its mindset on how it perceives mistakes and failures. Instead of viewing failures and mistakes as something to be avoided at all costs, which can lead to hiding them from others, it's healthier to approach them as valuable learning opportunities. To set the tone and create a safe space for others to share, I strongly recommend that the leader takes the lead in answering this question. By going first, the leader demonstrates vulnerability and openness, paving the way for team members to follow suit.

Question 4: What skills or areas of improvement are you trying to develop?

The final discussion question aims to enhance the team's ability to ask for help. A psychologically safe team is one where people are willing to be vulnerable and openly ask for help with things they are struggling with. The goal is to avoid a culture where people suffer in silence. Some team members might hesitate to ask for help because they believe their colleagues are too busy or because they don't want to be perceived as incompetent. Regardless of the reason, it's essential to foster a culture where teammates actively seek support when needed.

After the four questions, debrief the team:

The four questions are designed to initiate healthy conversations within the team, but they should not be the final action in building psychological safety. Talking is not enough; you need to take action based on the new information gathered. After answering these four questions as a team, discuss how you can use this newfound knowledge in practical terms:

How can you design tasks and responsibilities to use each other's strengths?

How can you tap into team members' underutilised strengths?

What steps will you take to ensure a culture where everyone feels comfortable asking for help?

How will the team discuss and learn from their mistakes?

By engaging in this facilitated discussion and taking action based on the insights gained, your team can make significant strides in building a psychologically safe environment where everyone feels valued, supported, and empowered to grow.

Chapter summary

In this chapter, we've explored the critical significance of psychological safety in bolstering team resilience. We explored the notion of interpersonal risk, shedding light on its potential drawbacks and underlining the necessity of creating an environment where individuals can freely express their thoughts, ideas, and concerns without apprehension of judgment or reprisal. Through a blend of real-life instances and personal narratives, we've showcased how psychological safety acts as a catalyst for encouraging open dialogue, embracing risk, learning from errors, building flexibility, promoting collaboration, and nurturing shared accountability. Additionally, the chapter offers an in-depth case study, demonstrating practical strategies for instilling psychological safety within teams, ultimately culminating in heightened resilience, innovation, and success.

Reflection

Reflect on instances where you've felt inhibited from expressing concerns or taking risks within your team. Consider the impact of such situations on open communication and collaboration.

Draw parallels between your experiences and success stories like Pixar and Unilever. Reflect on how psychological safety, or its absence, influenced creativity and innovation in your work environment.

Contemplate situations where fear of backlash or reprisal affects your decision-making. Consider how a psychologically unsafe environment can stifle growth and innovation.

Evaluate the role of learning from mistakes in your team or organisation. Reflect on how a culture of learning from failures contributes to resilience and continuous improvement.

Consider your team's adaptability to change. Consider how your team's capacity to overcome obstacles, bounce back from failures, and prosper in a fast-paced setting is affected by psychological safety.

Think about instances where psychological safety has contributed to individual and collective growth. Reflect on how shared responsibility and collaboration enhance team resilience.

Action

Actively encourage open dialogue within your team. Establish spaces where team members may voice their worries, exchange ideas, and offer feedback without worrying about criticism or reprisal.

Embrace vulnerability as a leader. Share personal stories of overcoming challenges to create a culture where team members feel comfortable sharing their own experiences.

Implement continuous empowerment strategies. Provide training and mentorship opportunities to equip team members with the skills and knowledge needed for active participation and decision-making.

Establish a systematic approach to learning from mistakes. Create regular sessions where team members can openly discuss setbacks, share insights, and collectively learn from experiences.

Facilitate structured open dialogue sessions. Encourage cross-functional brainstorming to enhance communication, exchange diverse perspectives, and foster innovation within the team.

Set up mechanisms for holistic acknowledgement of concerns. Formulate task forces to address systemic issues, ensuring that feedback from team members leads to tangible actions and continuous improvement.

PART THREE
DEVELOPING RESILIENT LEADERSHIP

CHAPTER FIVE:
CREATING RESILIENT LEADERSHIP

What you will gain from this chapter

Insights into the crucial role of leadership in developing organisational resilience, particularly during times of crisis or rapid change.

An awareness of the fundamental elements of resilient leadership, such as emotional control during times of change, role modelling, nurturing creativity, and leadership style.

An in-depth look at authentic leadership and its impact on team resilience, supported by research findings and practical steps to cultivate self-awareness, balanced processing, ethical standards, and transparency.

Knowledge of how social learning theory and the power of role modelling can shape a resilient team culture, with actionable guidance for implementing these principles effectively.

Strategies for creating a culture of creativity and embracing the concept of "failing fast" to promote resilience and adaptability within teams.

An appreciation for the importance of empathy, active listening, and support in navigating the emotional journey of change and creating resilient teams.

Insight: What has leadership got to do with it?

In earlier chapters on resilient processes, I shared an important experience from leading a commercial team for a yoghurt manufacturing business. The unexpected strike in our French factory, explored in depth in those pages, was a defining moment that tested the strength of the team and myself, as a leader. The principles discussed in that context, including swift assessment, strategic resource allocation, and transparent communication, laid the groundwork for navigating uncharted waters. Now, as we move on to the theme of resilient leadership, this personal story serves as an example. It was a period of crisis management, a test of adaptability, and a testament to the importance of creating a proactive and resilient team culture. The challenges presented by the strike demanded not just managerial skills but true leadership in the face of uncertainty. As we explore the realm of resilient leadership, let's revisit the lessons learned during those turbulent times. How did the team's cohesion and adaptability play a role? What leadership qualities were instrumental in steering through unforeseen disruptions? By referencing this personal story, we anchor ourselves in a real-world example that vividly illustrates the application of resilient processes and sets the stage for deeper insights into the dynamics of resilient leadership.

Since leadership is the cornerstone of organisational and team resilience, it is important to address resilient leadership in this book. In times of crisis or rapid change, the leader can inspire, guide, and empower their team to determine the organisation's ability to weather the storm and emerge stronger. By exploring the principles of resilient leadership, this chapter will equip you with actionable insights and strategies to cultivate resilience within your teams and organisations. Moreover, in a world marked by volatility, uncertainty, complexity, and ambiguity (VUCA), resilient leadership brings stability and guidance. As a result, this chapter's exploration of resilient leadership not only covers a crucial component of organisational success but also gives you vital tools to prosper in a constantly changing workplace environment. In the vast landscape of leadership literature, countless books offer insights into team management. However, my focus here is to explore specific leadership elements that have a profound influence on creating team resilience. Let's explore these key facets:

Leadership Style

How you lead shapes the team's dynamic. Adopting a resilient leadership style involves inspiring confidence, providing support, and leading by example. It's about steering the team with resilience as a core value, encouraging adaptability, and fostering a collective mindset to face challenges head-on.

» Role Modelling

Being resilient yourself is what makes a leader more influential than simply giving orders. The behaviour of a team is modelled by leaders, who hold significant influence. As a leader, you motivate your team to overcome obstacles head-on by modelling perseverance in the face of difficulty.

» Creativity and Failing Fast

Resilient teams thrive in an environment that encourages creativity and embraces the concept of "failing fast." Leaders who create an atmosphere of innovation and experimentation empower their teams to take calculated risks. This approach not only fuels creativity but also instils resilience by viewing setbacks as stepping stones to success.

» Emotional Management During Change

Change is a constant. Resilient leaders recognise the emotional impact of change on their teams. Managing these emotions involves empathy, active listening, and providing the necessary support. Leaders who navigate change with a focus on emotional well-being cultivate a resilient team ready to adapt and thrive.

In conclusion, while leadership literature offers a plethora of insights, honing in on these specific elements - leadership style, role modelling, creativity and emotional management during change - can profoundly influence your team's resilience. By integrating these practices into your leadership approach, you pave the way for a resilient, adaptive, and high-performing team.

Your leadership style

Understanding a leader's approach and style is vital due to the considerable impact leadership has on the dynamics and behaviour of a team inside an organisation (Rousseau et al., 2013). Leadership has such an impact on creating environments and cultures of innovation, collaboration and creative thinking, all of which are vital for creating and developing resilient teams and organisations. Several researchers have theorised that there is a link between leadership and resilience. Luthans and Avolio (2003), expressed that "authentic leadership created the capacity for team resilience." It was suggested by Sutcliffe and Vogus (2003), "that leadership had a positive role in helping employees adjust and adapt in challenging times." As part of my MSc in Psychology (Roberts, 2022), I researched the impact of leadership style on promoting team resilience and found that authentic leadership is highly correlated to increasing the resilience of a team.

Authentic leadership as a construct is grounded in positive psychology along with Positive Organisational Behaviour (POB). According to Harter (2002), the construct is considered to have originated from the ancient Greek philosophy "To thine own self be true," and it has become even more influential in the previous century (Erickson, 1995). Positive psychology literature (Cameron et al., 2003; Seligman, 2002) has enlarged the concept of authenticity by defining it as "owning one's inner experiences, be they thoughts, emotions, needs, wants, preferences, or beliefs, processes captured by the exhortation to know oneself" (Harter, 2002).

Ultimately, authenticity requires being conscious of and accepting responsibility for one's own life experiences, as well as exhibiting and being true to oneself. And because the current understanding of authentic leadership has its origins in POB and has been significantly developed within the context of organisations, this combination enhances both self-awareness and self-control. These two qualities, therefore, enable leaders to be more flexible and creative in their mental processes, allowing them to aid their staff in coping with hardship (Gardner & Schermerhorn, 2004). The definition of authentic leadership is "a pattern of leader behaviour that draws upon and promotes both positive psychological capacities and a positive ethical climate, to foster positive self-development by helping followers develop greater self-awareness, an internal moral perspective, balanced information processing, and relational transparency." (Walumbwa et al., 2008). Walumbwa et al. (2008) assert that authentic leadership consists of four dimensions: self-awareness, balanced processing, an internal moral perspective, and relational transparency.

Firstly, despite a long history of understanding, significant study on self-awareness has only recently—roughly in the last 50 years—been conducted (Duval & Silva, 2001). Duval and Silva (2001) hypothesised that conscious attention is focused on evaluating oneself. By turning our attention inward, we develop what Duval and Silva dubbed "objective self-awareness," which prompts us to evaluate our performance in light of known standards. A standard was defined as "a mental representation of correct behaviour, attitudes, and traits. All of the standards of correctness taken together define what a 'correct' person is" (Duval & Wicklund, 1972). Using this definition in the leadership context would suggest that a leader has a standard which must grow and improve to allow for continual self-improvement. Knowing who you are deeply, what drives you, what your strengths are, and where you need to grow to be a more effective leader while also being conscious of your influence on others are all aspects of self-awareness (Kernis, 2003).

Secondly, balanced processing is defined by Walumbwa et al. (2008) as "the capacity to process information from those around you and make a pertinent, sound judgement and relevant decision, ensuring you have elicited information from those around you". Group decision-making is a perfect example of this, since for a group to reach a consensus, they must all be committed to the decision. How we measure the meaning of the group consensus on a decision being made is based on the personal commitment of each team member's feeling towards that decision. This would imply that an authentic leader is aware of each team member's feelings when making group decisions (Ellis & Fisher, 1994).

Thirdly, with organisations' drive to deliver profit targets, many leaders will do anything to achieve this and appear to have a low priority for ethics and moral behaviour (Serra-Garcia, van Damme & Potters, 2011). Making sure that leaders adhere to their values and ideals in relation to the outside world while also upholding a standard of ethics, professionalism, and integrity is known as having an internal moral perspective (Avolio & Gardner, 2005; Walumbwa et al., 2008). There are similarities to objective self-awareness, as authentic leaders must have a clear ethical standard to compare themselves and make sure their decision-making is congruent with their values and beliefs.

And fourthly, there is pressure for leaders to be open and transparent. Much of the reason for this transparency comes from corporate scandals, where confidence has been eroded for both employees and shareholders of the company, hence the need for openness and transparency. There has been a suggestion that authentic leadership has similarities to transformational leadership since transformational leaders look to inspire their followers, but not always from a place of authenticity, since what they inspire may not be what they practice themselves (Bass & Steidhneier, 1999). Authentic leaders will be true to their words, deeds, and principles, and this must be transparent to their followers. Additionally, relationship openness ensures that followers see their actual thoughts and emotions when appropriate, helping to embed and build trust (Gardner et al., 2005).

There are several aspects that authentic leadership impacts within organisations. Building follower efficacy is the first. This is done by the leader instilling confidence and trust in their team which results in their teams understanding their capabilities (Gardner & Schermerhorn, 2004). Secondly, authentic leadership inspires optimism. High-hope individuals are more likely to be challenged by their own goals, to place a higher value on achieving their goals, and to be more adaptable to change to do so, according to Luthans (2002). They are also more able to form interdependent bonds and maintain emotional equilibrium under pressure. Studies also showed that leaders with higher hopes tended to have more profitable organisations, more fulfilled employees, and a lower staff turnover (Gardner & Schermerhorn, 2004).

My approach to leadership is rooted in authenticity, especially during times of crisis. When I found myself navigating the challenges within my role as commercial leader of the yoghurt business, I approached it with a commitment to genuine and transparent leadership. Authentic leadership, to me, means leading with integrity, empathy, and honesty. During the crisis, I made it a priority to communicate openly with my team, sharing both the successes and the setbacks we faced. I believed in being transparent about the situation we were in and the steps we needed to take to address it. During this time, we encountered supply chain disruptions that threatened our production capabilities. Instead of sugar-coating the situation or placing blame, I gathered my team together and openly discussed the challenges we were facing. I acknowledged their concerns, listened to their input, and worked collaboratively to find solutions. Additionally, authentic leadership involves leading by example. In the face of uncertainty and adversity, I remained calm, demonstrating resilience and optimism to inspire my team. I encouraged open dialogue and welcomed feedback, creating a culture where everyone felt valued and empowered to contribute their ideas. I prioritised empathy, recognising that my team members were navigating their challenges amidst the crisis. I made an effort to check in with each individual, offering support and understanding where needed.

By demonstrating empathy and compassion, I fostered a sense of camaraderie and unity within the team, strengthening our collective resilience. Overall, my approach to leadership during the crisis was guided by authenticity, transparency, and empathy. By leading from an authentic place and embodying these values, I was able to navigate the challenges we faced with integrity and resilience, ultimately leading the business through the crisis and emerging stronger as a team. Authentic leadership is essential for resilient teams and organisations because resilient organisations are hopeful ones, grounded on the realistic assessment of any obstacles in one's environment but also in one's ability to overcome these challenges (Groopman, 2004).

In my Psychology Master's thesis, I conducted a comprehensive study involving a sample of 95 employees from diverse global organisations, all belonging to teams of three or more members.

The results revealed a robust and statistically significant correlation between authentic leadership and team resilience ($r = 0.712$; $p < 0.01$). Furthermore, the research indicated that authentic leadership serves as a positive predictor of team resilience. Taking a closer look at the four sub-dimensions of authentic leadership, the analysis highlighted internal moral perspective and self-awareness as particularly influential factors in predicting team resilience. While the multifaceted nature of authentic leadership is well-established, these findings underscore the distinct psychological functions of each sub-dimension, with a specific focus on the pivotal roles played by self-awareness and internal moral perspective. These insights contribute to a deeper understanding of how authentic leadership influences and nurtures resilience within teams.

How do we create an authentic approach to leadership?

In the journey towards building team resilience, the role of authentic leadership stands out as a powerful influence. Here are some practical steps that you can take to embody authentic leadership, drawing inspiration from real-life examples.

1. Cultivate Self-Awareness

To embark on the journey of authentic leadership and create team resilience, leaders must first cultivate self-awareness—an intimate understanding of your thoughts, emotions, and behaviours. Here's how you can integrate self-awareness into your leadership practice:

» Action: Schedule regular reflective time

In the hustle and bustle of leadership responsibilities, it's easy to lose sight of introspection. However, carving out dedicated time for self-reflection is paramount. Block off a portion of your schedule, whether it's a few minutes each day or a designated hour each week, to pause, ponder, and probe into your inner landscape.

Implementation: Consider a dedicated weekly "reflection

hour" to delve into personal reactions, decisions, and areas for growth. Set aside a sacred hour each week—a sanctuary for introspection and self-discovery. During this time, retreat to a quiet space free from distractions. Reflect on recent interactions, decisions made, and challenges faced. Explore your emotional responses, interrogate your thought patterns, and identify areas for personal and professional growth.

This intentional practice of self-reflection serves as a mirror, illuminating facets of your leadership style and shedding light on blind spots. It enhances self-awareness, empowering you to navigate leadership complexities with clarity and purpose. As you embark on this journey of self-discovery, remember that self-awareness is not a destination but a continuous voyage of exploration. Embrace the discomfort of self-examination, celebrate moments of insight, and remain open to the transformative power of self-awareness in your leadership journey.

2. Promote Balanced Processing

In the quest for authentic leadership and the cultivation of team resilience, promoting balanced processing is a pivotal step. This involves actively seeking diverse perspectives during decision-making to ensure a comprehensive and well-rounded approach. Here's how you can integrate balanced processing into your leadership practice:

» Action: Actively seek diverse perspectives during decision-making

Embrace the richness that diverse viewpoints bring to the decision-making table. Actively seek out input from individuals with varying experiences, expertise, and perspectives. Recognise that the collective wisdom of a diverse team often leads to more robust and innovative solutions.

Implementation: Before making crucial decisions, gather your team for a brainstorming session.

Visualise a scenario where you are faced with a critical decision that will impact the team and organisation. Instead of relying solely on your insights, you orchestrate a collaborative brainstorming session. Bringing together team members from different departments, levels, and backgrounds, you then create an inclusive space for diverse voices to be heard.

By incorporating various viewpoints, you ensure decisions are well-rounded and reflective of collective wisdom. During the brainstorming session, you encourage open dialogue, inviting team members to share their perspectives, concerns, and creative ideas. This inclusive approach ensures that the decision-making process is enriched by the collective intelligence of the team. You actively listen, value dissenting opinions, and create an environment where everyone feels empowered to contribute. In this way, the implementation of balanced processing transforms decision-making from a solitary act to a collaborative endeavour. You become a facilitator of collective wisdom, resulting in decisions that are not only well-informed but also resonate with the diverse values and experiences of the entire team. This approach not only enhances the quality of decisions but also strengthens the team's cohesion and adaptability in the face of challenges.

3. Uphold Ethical Standards

In the realm of authentic leadership and the nurturing of team resilience, upholding ethical standards is a cornerstone. It involves not just articulating but consistently embodying the values that define an organisation's moral compass. Here's how you can integrate the commitment to ethical standards into your leadership practice:

» Action: Articulate and consistently uphold organisational values

Begin by clearly defining and articulating the core values that underpin your organisation's identity. These values serve as the guiding principles that shape decision-making, behaviour, and the overall culture. Ensure that these values are not mere slogans but resonate as the heartbeat of your organisational ethos.

Implementation: Ensure you frequently communicate the

company's core values, both in internal discussions and public forums.

Ensure that you embody the organisation's values in every aspect of your leadership journey. You become a vocal advocate for these values, consistently communicating them in various settings—be it internal team discussions, public forums, or interactions with stakeholders.

Ensure that ethical considerations are at the forefront of decision-making, creating an atmosphere of integrity in the team. When faced with decisions, consciously weigh the options against the backdrop of the organisation's values. Ethical considerations become non-negotiable elements in the decision-making process. Your commitment to integrity sets a powerful example for the team, creating a culture where ethical conduct is not just encouraged but expected. By consistently upholding organisational values, you create a sense of purpose and unity within the team. Team members understand that their actions align with a broader ethical framework, instilling a shared sense of responsibility. This commitment to ethical standards not only enhances the team's resilience but also fortifies its reputation and trustworthiness in the broader organisational context. In essence, ethical leadership becomes key in building a resilient team that thrives on a foundation of integrity.

4. Embrace Transparency

In the landscape of authentic leadership and the cultivation of team resilience, embracing transparency emerges as a catalyst for trust and cohesion. It involves the open sharing of thoughts, emotions, and the rationale behind decisions. Here's how you can weave transparency into your leadership:

» Action: Share thoughts, emotions, and decision-making rationale openly

Begin by recognising that transparency is not just about revealing facts but also about conveying the thought processes and emotions that underpin your decisions. Cultivate a mindset that values open communication and embraces vulnerability as a strength.

Implementation: Consider yourself in various situations such as during team meetings, openly discussing challenges faced and the decision-making process behind key choices.

Ensure you embody transparency by encouraging a culture of open dialogue. In team meetings, take the opportunity to share both successes and challenges authentically. This transparency builds trust, as team members witness your authenticity and commitment to open communication. By openly sharing the decision-making rationale, you invite the team into the decision-making arena. This not only demystifies leadership choices but also builds a sense of inclusivity. Team members witness your authenticity, realising that transparency is not a mere buzzword but a lived value.

In this environment of openness, trust becomes a cornerstone. Team members feel secure in knowing that they are privy to the reasoning behind decisions, even in challenging times. Your commitment to transparent communication creates an environment where honesty is not just encouraged but expected. This, in turn, fortifies the team's resilience, creating a collective strength grounded in trust and mutual understanding. Embracing transparency is not merely a leadership action; it becomes a guiding principle that shapes a resilient team's identity and strength.

By weaving in these daily leadership practices, you can become the living embodiment of authentic leadership. This, in turn, shapes resilient teams and organisations, creating an environment where adaptability, trust, and collective strength thrive in the face of challenges. In the pursuit of team resilience, authentic leadership is not just a concept—it's a transformative force guiding leaders towards enduring success.

The power of role modelling

Role modelling is a powerful influence that shapes behaviours, attitudes, and values within a team. Rooted in social learning theory, which was extensively explored by psychologist Albert Bandura, role modelling involves observing, imitating, and internalising the behaviours of role models in one's environment. Richard Searle, Managing Director and Head of Advisory at BDO Limited Guernsey, highlights the significance of role modelling by stating that even minor actions, such as leaders demonstrating attentiveness to well-being, hold the potential to impact the team's behaviour and perceptions profoundly.

Albert Bandura's "Bobo doll experiments" conducted in the early 1960s (Bandura, 1962) were ground-breaking studies that significantly contributed to the understanding of social learning theory and the influential role of role modelling in shaping behaviour. The experiments were designed to investigate how individuals, particularly children, learn new behaviours through observation and imitation of others. The findings from these experiments laid the foundation for Bandura's social cognitive theory.

In these experiments, Bandura and his colleagues exposed children to different scenarios involving an inflatable doll named Bobo. The key elements of the experiments were as follows:

Aggressive modelling: Children observed an adult model displaying aggressive behaviour towards the Bobo doll, such as hitting, kicking, and using aggressive language. The adult model demonstrated these behaviours in a controlled environment.

Non-aggressive modelling: Another group of children observed an adult model who did not display any aggressive behaviour towards the Bobo doll. This group served as a control to compare the effects of aggressive modelling.

Observational learning: After observing the adult model, the children were then placed in a room with the Bobo doll and other toys. Researchers observed the children's behaviour to determine if they would imitate the modelled aggressive actions.

The findings from Bandura's experiments were profound and challenged prevailing behaviourist theories that emphasised the role of reinforcement in learning. The key conclusions drawn from the Bobo doll experiments were:

Observational learning: Children who witnessed the aggressive model were more likely to imitate the observed behaviours when allowed to interact with the Bobo doll. This demonstrated that learning could occur through observation alone.

Imitation and modelling: The children not only imitated the specific aggressive actions that they observed but also replicated the general pattern of aggressive behaviour displayed by the adult model.

Role of reinforcement: Bandura found that reinforcement played a role in influencing the likelihood of imitation. If children observed the adult model being rewarded or praised for the aggressive behaviour, they were more inclined to imitate it.

These experiments highlighted the significance of role modelling in shaping behaviour and challenged behaviourist notions that emphasised the exclusive role of reinforcement in learning. Bandura's social cognitive theory proposed that individuals learn not just through direct experience but also through observing and imitating others, emphasising the cognitive processes involved in learning and behaviour acquisition. The findings of the Bobo doll experiments have had a lasting impact on the fields of psychology, education, and leadership, influencing our understanding of how individuals learn and adapt behaviours through social observation.

In the context of leadership and resilience, you can draw specific insights from Albert Bandura's learnings to create a resilient culture within your teams:

Model resilient responses

Drawing from Bandura's insights on observational learning, we explore how leaders can model resilient responses to challenges, setting the tone for their teams' navigation through difficulties. Bandura's experiments underscore the power of observed behaviours in shaping individual actions. As leaders, we must lead by example, showcasing composure, adaptability, and a positive outlook in the face of adversity. By modelling resilient responses to challenges, we set the tone for our teams and inspire them to navigate difficulties with confidence and resilience.

Consistency in resilience display

Consistency is key when it comes to reinforcing behaviours. By routinely exhibiting resilient behaviours, whether in the face of minor setbacks or major crises, we reinforce the expectation of resilience within our teams. This consistency establishes a solid foundation for a culture of resilience to thrive and become ingrained in our organisations.

Positive reinforcement for resilient efforts

Bandura's research highlights the influence of reinforcement on behaviour. As leaders, we must actively recognise and acknowledge resilient efforts within our teams. Providing positive reinforcement not only stresses the importance of resilience but also encourages its continued display, ultimately shaping a resilient organisational culture. By incorporating these insights, as a leader you can play a pivotal role in shaping a resilient culture within your teams, where adaptive responses to challenges become ingrained in the organisational DNA.

Creativity and failing fast

As a leader dedicated to building team resilience, creating a culture of creativity, and embracing the concept of "failing fast", is paramount. A creative culture is one where innovation is celebrated, ideas are welcomed, and team members feel empowered to think outside the box. Encouraging an environment where creativity flourishes not only enhances problem-solving but also instils a sense of ownership and pride among team members. Such an environment is created through psychological safety, as discussed in an earlier chapter. Organisations such as Google exemplify this approach, with their famous "20% time" policy allowing employees to dedicate a portion of their workweek to pursue personal projects, which has led to breakthrough innovations.

Embracing the notion of "failing fast" involves creating a safe space where experimentation is encouraged, and setbacks are viewed as opportunities for learning and improvement.

Companies like Amazon, through initiatives like their internal "Failures of the Week" meetings, acknowledge and dissect failures openly, extracting valuable lessons and insights. This approach not only destigmatises failure but also cultivates a resilient mindset among team members, emphasising that setbacks are a natural part of the creative process. Linking these practices to team resilience, a creative culture, and the acceptance of failure, contribute to the development of adaptive and agile teams. When individuals feel secure in expressing their ideas and are not afraid of failure, they become more resilient in the face of challenges. This resilience stems from the team's ability to pivot, innovate, and view setbacks as stepping stones toward eventual success. By creating such a culture, leaders play an important role in not only enhancing team creativity but also in fortifying the team's collective resilience.

Another principle to creating a creative and "failing fast" environment is to lead by example. This entails demonstrating a willingness to take calculated risks and openly acknowledging mistakes. Leadership sets the tone for establishing such a culture. Leading by example is crucial, as demonstrated by leaders like Elon Musk, who openly acknowledges Tesla's failures in its journey toward electric vehicle dominance. Musk's willingness to take risks and learn from mistakes inspires his team to do the same. Amazon's "Day 1" philosophy emphasises constant innovation and a willingness to experiment, even if it means failure. Founder Jeff Bezos famously said, "Failure and invention are inseparable twins." This mindset has allowed Amazon to continually push boundaries and disrupt industries.

Providing resources and support is another critical aspect. Companies invest heavily in employee development programs, encouraging continuous learning and skill development. This investment enables employees to explore new ideas and push the boundaries of innovation. Moreover, celebrating creativity is essential for reinforcing its value within the organisation. Pixar Animation Studios is known for its ground-breaking films, creating an environment where creative collaboration is celebrated, and ideas are welcomed from all levels of the organisation. Establishing a learning culture encourages continuous growth and resilience. Companies like Microsoft promote a growth mindset among their employees, promoting a culture where learning from failures is embraced as part of the journey toward success. Recognising that the first iteration of an idea may not be perfect allows for multiple rounds of refinement. This approach is exemplified by companies like Apple, which continuously improve products based on user feedback and technological advancements.

Promoting cross-functional collaboration is another key strategy for nurturing creativity and resilience within teams. Collaborative efforts involving individuals from different departments often result in more diverse perspectives and innovative solutions. For instance, companies like Airbnb facilitate cross-functional teams to develop new features or address complex challenges. Establishing a supportive feedback system is essential for creating a culture of continuous improvement and resilience.

By consistently implementing these strategies, leaders can create a dynamic and resilient team culture that thrives on creativity, collaboration, and continuous improvement.

We have emotions

As a reminder of the transformative power of emotional management in leadership, let me take you back to an important moment in my career: the supply crisis that affected the yoghurt business where I served as the commercial team leader. Amidst the chaos and uncertainty, I discovered invaluable lessons about the impact of empathy, active listening, and unwavering support within my team. These experiences have since become foundational principles in my approach to leadership, guiding me in building resilience and adaptability within my teams.

Empathy became increasingly important in my approach. By connecting with each team member on a human level and understanding their fears, concerns, and aspirations, I cultivated a culture of compassion and solidarity. Our shared experiences during this crisis forged a bond that transcended professional roles, uniting us in our collective resolve to overcome adversity. Active listening also emerged as a powerful tool. Through genuine, attentive listening, I gained insights into the nuanced emotions underlying the team's reactions to the crisis. This allowed me to address their concerns openly, transparently, and with empathy, creating a climate of trust and mutual respect. I ensured that they had the resources, guidance, and encouragement needed to navigate the challenges ahead. By creating a supportive infrastructure and empowering my team to confront obstacles head-on, we emerged from the crisis stronger and more resilient. In hindsight, the lessons learned from this experience have profoundly shaped my leadership philosophy. Today, I approach every challenge with a deep appreciation for the emotional journey that accompanies change. By embracing empathy, active listening, and steadfast support, I strive to cultivate resilient teams capable of weathering any storm.

Understanding the Change Curve

The change curve, originally developed by Elisabeth Kubler-Ross in the 1960s, often represented as a series of emotional stages including denial, resistance, exploration, and commitment, illustrates the psychological responses individuals undergo during change. Resilient leaders recognise that team members may traverse this curve at different paces and that addressing emotional needs is crucial at each stage.

Denial stage: Individuals resist the idea of change and may refuse to acknowledge its necessity or potential impact. They may exhibit behaviours such as ignoring information about the change, minimising its significance, or expressing disbelief in its validity.

Resistance stage: Individuals start to confront the reality of change and experience negative emotions such as anger, frustration, or anxiety. They may resist the change actively by expressing opposition, questioning its rationale, or even sabotaging its implementation.

Exploration stage: Individuals begin to explore the implications of the change and seek ways to adapt. They may experiment with new ideas, processes, or behaviours, and start to accept the need for change. However, they may still experience uncertainty or hesitation about fully embracing the change.

Commitment stage: Individuals fully embrace the change and commit to making it work. They demonstrate readiness to adapt, actively engage in the change process, and contribute to its success. They may exhibit behaviours such as enthusiasm, collaboration, and resilience in overcoming challenges associated with the change.

How Resilient Leaders Can Navigate the Change Curve:

» Denial stage:

Recognise signs: Individuals may exhibit behaviours such as ignoring or dismissing the need for change, clinging to the status quo, or denying the severity of the situation.

Approach with empathy: Understand that denial is a natural response to change and acknowledge the validity of team members' feelings. Offer support and reassurance while gently challenging misconceptions.

Provide information: Share clear and compelling reasons for the change, addressing any misconceptions or fears that contribute to denial. Encourage open dialogue and questions to facilitate understanding.

» Resistance stage:

Acknowledge concerns: Individuals may express frustration, anger, or scepticism towards the proposed changes. Listen actively to concerns and validate emotions without judgment.

Communicate benefits: Highlight the benefits and opportunities that the change brings, emphasising how it aligns with organisational goals and individual aspirations. Address specific concerns and misconceptions to alleviate resistance.

Involve and empower: Involve team members in the change process by seeking their input, addressing their concerns, and empowering them to contribute to solutions. Provide opportunities for collaboration and ownership to foster buy-in.

» Exploration stage:

Encourage experimentation: As individuals move into the exploration stage, they begin to accept the need for change and explore new possibilities. Encourage experimentation and creativity, allowing team members to test new ideas and approaches.

Provide support: Offer resources, training, and guidance to support team members as they explore new ways of working. Provide feedback and encouragement to reinforce progress and build confidence.

Support learning: Emphasise the importance of continuous learning and adaptation during the exploration stage. Encourage reflection upon successes and failures, extracting valuable lessons to inform future efforts.

» **Commitment stage:**

Celebrate progress: Acknowledge when individuals fully embrace the change and commit to its success. Celebrate milestones and achievements, recognising the hard work and dedication of team members.

Reinforce values: Reinforce the organisation's values and vision, highlighting how the change aligns with shared goals and aspirations. Encourage a sense of purpose and pride in contributing to something meaningful.

Sustain momentum: Maintain momentum by embedding the change into the organisation's culture and processes. Continuously monitor progress, address any remaining challenges, and adapt as needed to ensure long-term success.

By understanding and effectively navigating the stages of the change curve, as a resilient leader you can support your teams through the emotional journey of change, ultimately creating resilience, growth, and success.

An exemplary illustration of navigating the change curve is evident in the leadership demonstrated by Tim Cook during Apple's transition from traditional product-focused strategies to a more services-oriented approach. Similarly, during the crisis I faced in the yoghurt business, resilient leadership played an important role in managing the challenges and steering the company towards stability. Just as Cook emphasised transparent communication at Apple, I prioritised open and honest dialogue with my team, ensuring that everyone understood the gravity of the situation. Additionally, providing resources for skill development became essential in both contexts, as employees needed to adapt to new roles and responsibilities. Moreover, just as Apple adapted to market changes, I remained flexible and agile in my decision-making processes, responding quickly to emerging challenges. Finally, celebrating incremental successes, no matter how small, boosted morale and motivated teams to persevere through adversity, both in the tech industry and the yoghurt business. Overall, these leadership strategies contributed to the resilience and eventual success of both organisations amidst significant transitions and crises.

In summary, resilient leaders not only comprehend the change curve but actively engage with it. By creating open communication, providing guidance, demonstrating flexibility, and celebrating achievements, leaders contribute to a resilient team that not only embraces change but emerges stronger on the other side of transformation.

Chapter summary

Resilient leadership empowers individuals and teams to thrive amidst challenges and uncertainties. It is anchored in emotional intelligence, strategic vision, empowerment, and a culture of proactive problem-solving. Resilient leadership encompasses leadership style, role modelling, fostering creativity, and embracing failure. With a focus on clear communication and emotional management during change, we've emphasised the importance of authentic leadership, drawing insights from research and offering practical steps to cultivate self-awareness, balanced processing, ethical standards, and transparency. From Bandura's social learning theory, we've highlighted the influential power of role modelling in shaping a resilient team culture, providing actionable guidance for you to implement these principles effectively. We have also looked at how to manage emotions in the team with the change curve, which outlines the emotional stages individuals experience during transitions: denial, resistance, exploration, and commitment.

Reflection

Reflect on the profound impact leadership has on team dynamics and organisational culture. Consider how your leadership style influences the resilience and adaptability of your team.

Explore the concept of authentic leadership and its role in fostering resilience. Reflect on your ability to lead authentically; considering how self-awareness, transparency, and ethical standards shape your leadership approach.

Reflect on your experiences navigating change and uncertainty within your organisation. Consider how your leadership style has contributed to building resilience and guiding your team through challenging times.

Reflect on your ability to lead by example and model resilient behaviours for your team. Consider how your actions and attitudes influence team culture and resilience, and reflect on ways to demonstrate adaptability, positivity, and perseverance.

Contemplate the concept of "failing fast" and its role in promoting resilience. Reflect on your attitudes towards failure and how creating a safe space for experimentation can lead to valuable learning experiences and eventual success.

Reflect on your experiences navigating the change curve and supporting your team through periods of transition and uncertainty. Consider how acknowledging and addressing the emotional stages of change contributes to team resilience and success.

Action

Dedicate regular time for self-reflection to deepen your understanding of your leadership style and its impact on team resilience.

Actively seek input from team members with diverse backgrounds and experiences during decision-making processes to promote inclusivity and balanced processing.

Create opportunities for open dialogue and communication during team meetings, encouraging team members to voice their perspectives and concerns openly.

Prioritise empathy in your leadership approach, actively listening to team members' concerns and providing support and understanding during challenging times.

Creating a culture of experimentation by providing time, resources, and support for team members to explore new ideas and approaches.

Anticipate and address the emotional stages of change within your team or organisation, providing empathy, support, and clear communication throughout the process.

CHAPTER SIX:
CREATING DIVERSITY AND INCLUSION

What you will gain from this chapter

Insights into how diverse perspectives and thought processes within a team can help navigate complexities and find effective solutions when faced with challenges.

Understanding of the compelling reasons why diversity is essential for building team resilience, supported by real-world examples and research-backed facts.

Knowledge of how diverse teams lead to innovative solutions, enhance adaptability and resilience, promote inclusivity and psychological safety, better represent and understand diverse customers, and attract and retain top talent.

Awareness of the importance of neurodiversity in building resilient teams and how embracing different ways of thinking and problem-solving strengthens a team's ability to adapt and thrive.

Strategies to combat groupthink and foster a more inclusive, diverse, and resilient decision-making process within teams.

A step-by-step guide on building a diverse and inclusive team, including self-reflection, setting clear goals, revamping recruitment practices, and encouraging an inclusive team culture.

Insights into the concepts of diversity, inclusion, and belonging, and their pivotal roles in creating a robust and adaptive team environment that can navigate challenges and thrive in the face of adversity.

Insight: What has diversity and inclusion got to do with building resilient teams?

As a leader of a yoghurt business, I faced a significant challenge when confronted with short supply and at times no supply for my customers. During challenging times, having diverse perspectives and thought processes within the team becomes invaluable in navigating the complexities and finding effective solutions. When we encounter challenges, we naturally rely on our current way of thinking to devise solutions. However, the nature of certain challenges may require a different approach, a fresh perspective that goes beyond our usual problem-solving methods. This is where the power of diversity truly shines. By surrounding ourselves with individuals who bring diverse experiences, backgrounds, and ways of thinking to the table, we gain access to a broader range of ideas and approaches. These unique perspectives can help us break free from our mental constraints and explore innovative solutions that we may not have considered otherwise.

In the face of adversity, a diverse team can offer a multitude of viewpoints, allowing us to examine the problem from various angles and uncover potential solutions that may have been overlooked. The collective intelligence and creativity that emerges from a diverse group can be a game-changer in overcoming obstacles and building resilience. Additionally, diversity promotes an inclusive and cooperative culture, where every team member feels valued and empowered to contribute their unique insights. This sense of belonging and shared purpose strengthens the team's ability to weather storms and bounce back from setbacks. In essence, embracing diversity is not just a matter of social responsibility; it is a strategic imperative for building resilient teams. By actively seeking out and leveraging the power of diverse perspectives, leaders can equip their teams with the adaptability, creativity, and collective strength needed to thrive in the face of any challenge.

Diversity is more than just meeting quotas or adhering to company or industry targets; it is a vital catalyst for creating resilient teams and driving significant business success. Rather than focusing on tokenism, recognising the profound impact of diversity on team resilience and organisational performance is essential. Numerous compelling reasons underscore the critical role diversity plays in building strong teams and achieving far-reaching positive outcomes for businesses.

Diverse perspectives lead to innovative solutions

A study by Boston Consulting Group found that companies with more diverse management teams generate 19% higher revenue due to innovation (Lorenzo et al., 2018). Allegra Chapman, a diversity and inclusion expert, and Co-Creator of Watch This Sp_ce, who I spoke with on my podcast - Helping Organisations Thrive, emphasises the importance of diversity in building resilient teams:

"When a team consists of individuals with varied backgrounds, perspectives, frames of reference and experiences, they collectively possess a broader awareness of potential pitfalls and challenges. Their diverse knowledge and insights allow them to anticipate and address issues more effectively, drawing from a wider range of expertise and understanding."

Diversity enhances adaptability and resilience

In today's rapidly changing business landscape, adaptability is a key component of resilience. Diverse teams are better equipped to adapt to new circumstances and challenges because they can draw upon a wide range of experiences and perspectives. McKinsey & Company, a global management consulting firm, has conducted extensive research on the impact of diversity on business performance. In their 2020 report "Diversity Wins: How Inclusion Matters," they found that companies in the top quartile for gender diversity on executive teams were 25% more likely to have above-average profitability than companies in the fourth quartile (Dixon-Fyle et al., 2020). This adaptability translates into improved business performance and resilience in the face of adversity. Allegra Chapman highlights how diverse teams are better equipped to handle crises: "Diverse teams are much more able to move through crises effectively. They are usually able to see a crisis coming a lot sooner than less diverse teams and cope much better when a crisis presents itself. Diverse teams recover better afterwards, and tend to implement better learnings than a less diverse team."

Diversity promotes inclusivity and psychological safety

When teams are diverse and inclusive, they create an environment where every member feels valued, respected, and empowered to contribute. This sense of psychological safety is crucial for building resilience, as it allows individuals to express themselves freely, take risks, and learn from failures. Google's Project Aristotle, a study on team effectiveness, found that psychological safety was the most important factor in determining team success (Duhigg, 2016). By creating inclusivity and psychological safety through diversity, teams can create a strong foundation for resilience and high performance. Allegra Chapman emphasises the importance of inclusion alongside diversity: "If there isn't inclusion, and people don't feel included, psychologically safe or motivated to contribute then you won't be able to reap the benefits of their diverse insights and contributions."

Diverse teams better represent and understand diverse customers

In an increasingly globalised and interconnected world, businesses serve diverse customer bases. Having a diverse team that reflects the diversity of the customer population enables organisations to better understand and meet the needs of their customers. A study by the Center for Talent Innovation found that companies with diverse teams are 70% more likely to capture new markets (Hewlett et al., 2013). By leveraging the insights and cultural competencies of diverse team members, organisations can build stronger connections with their customers, leading to increased resilience and business success.

Diversity attracts and retains top talent

Organisations that prioritise diversity and inclusion are more attractive to top talent, particularly among younger generations who value working in diverse and inclusive environments. A survey by Glassdoor found that 67% of job seekers consider diversity an important factor when evaluating companies and job offers (Glassdoor, 2020). By building diverse and inclusive teams, organisations can attract and retain the best talent.

The benefits of diversity and inclusion

The importance of diversity and inclusion in the workplace has gained significant attention in recent years, with numerous studies and thought leaders highlighting the tangible benefits for businesses. Creating a diverse and inclusive work environment has been shown to drive innovation, improve financial performance, and enhance overall organisational success. Let's explore some compelling evidence and perspectives from industry leaders and researchers:

As mentioned previously, McKinsey & Company found that companies in the top quartile for gender diversity on executive teams were 25% more likely to have above-average profitability than companies in the fourth quartile. In a similar vein, businesses that were in the top quartile for ethnic and cultural diversity had a 36% increase in profitability over those in the fourth quartile. Sundar Pichai, CEO of Google and Alphabet, emphasises the importance of fostering a culture of belonging and inclusivity. In a blog post, he stated, "To build products that work for everyone, we need a diversity of perspectives and experiences in our own workforce. That's why we continue to make diversity, equity, and inclusion a company-wide commitment and priority."

Accenture, a global professional services company, has made significant strides in promoting diversity and inclusion. Their "Getting to Equal 2020" report found that a culture of equality, where employees feel a sense of belonging and are valued for their unique contributions, is a powerful multiplier of innovation and growth. Companies with a robust culture of equality are more likely to have employees who are innovative and bring new ideas to the table.

Salesforce, a global leader in customer relationship management (CRM) software, has made equality a core value of its company culture. They have implemented various initiatives to promote diversity and inclusion, such as their "Equality Groups" which provide support and resources for underrepresented communities within the company. Salesforce CEO Marc Benioff has stated, "Equality is a core value at Salesforce, and we believe that businesses can be powerful platforms for social change." Harvard Business Review (HBR) has published numerous articles on the benefits of diversity and inclusion in the workplace. In one article titled "How Diversity Can Drive Innovation," authors Sylvia Ann Hewlett, Melinda Marshall, and Laura Sherbin discuss how diverse teams can lead to better problem-solving and increased creativity. They found that employees who feel included and valued for their unique perspectives are more likely to speak up and share ideas, leading to more innovative solutions.

What about neurodiversity?

Neurodiversity, which encompasses the different ways people's brains work, process information, and interact with the world, is a crucial aspect of diversity that can significantly contribute to building resilient teams. By embracing neurodiversity in the workplace, organisations can tap into a wealth of unique perspectives, skills, and problem-solving approaches that strengthen their teams' ability to adapt and overcome challenges.

Neurodivergent individuals often bring different ways of thinking and problem-solving to the table. For example, autistic individuals may excel at pattern recognition, attention to detail, and logical reasoning; while those with ADHD may be highly creative, innovative, and adaptable (Austin & Pisano, 2017). These diverse approaches to tackling challenges can help teams develop more comprehensive and effective solutions, enhancing their resilience in the face of complex problems. Neurodivergent team members can contribute to a team's adaptability and innovation by offering fresh perspectives and unconventional ideas. As Allegra Chapman points out in our conversation on my podcast – Helping Organisations Thrive, "Different thinking and perspectives, ways of approaching problems and different approaches to communication are all incredibly beneficial to a team. It makes a team much stronger." By creating an environment that values and leverages these differences, teams can become more agile, creative, and resilient in the face of change.

Creating an inclusive environment that welcomes and supports neurodiversity can contribute to psychological safety within a team. When neurodivergent individuals feel valued, respected, and able to bring their authentic selves to work, they are more likely to engage, contribute, and collaborate effectively (Edmondson, 2018). Neurodivergent individuals often possess unique strengths and skills that can complement those of their neurotypical colleagues. For example, an autistic team member's attention to detail and logical reasoning can pair well with a neurotypical colleague's strong communication and interpersonal skills. By identifying and building on these complementary strengths, teams can become more well-rounded, adaptable, and resilient. The presence of neurodivergent individuals on a team can help challenge assumptions and biases, encouraging team members to question the status quo and consider alternative approaches. This can lead to more robust decision-making, innovation, and problem-solving, all of which contribute to a team's resilience. To harness the benefits of neurodiversity for team resilience, organisations must actively create inclusive environments that support and value neurodivergent individuals. This includes providing accommodations such as flexible work arrangements, quiet spaces, and clear communication channels, as well as creating an environment that celebrates differences and encourages open dialogue. By doing so, organisations can build teams that are not only diverse but also highly resilient, adaptable, and equipped to thrive in the face of challenges.

Employers should focus on creating a space that works for everyone, rather than trying to accommodate each individual instance of neurodivergence. As an example of universal design principles that make a workplace neurodiversity friendly, Microsoft has implemented an Autism Hiring Program, which includes a more inclusive interview process, job coaching, and support for managers to create a more welcoming and accommodating work environment for autistic employees (Microsoft, 2021). By embracing neurodiversity and leveraging the unique strengths of each team member, organisations can create resilient teams that are greater than the sum of their parts.

Combatting groupthink

Groupthink is a psychological phenomenon that occurs within a group of people when the desire for harmony or conformity leads to dysfunctional decision-making outcomes. In a groupthink situation, members of the group tend to minimise conflict and reach a consensus without critically evaluating alternative viewpoints, often leading to irrational or suboptimal decisions.

Irving Janis, a social psychologist who popularised the term, identified eight symptoms of groupthink:

Illusion of invulnerability

Belief in the inherent morality of the group

Rationalisation of warnings

Stereotyping of out-groups

Self-censorship

Illusion of unanimity

Direct pressure on dissenters

Self-appointed mind guards

As a leader, there are several strategies you can employ to overcome groupthink and create a more inclusive, diverse, and resilient decision-making process:

Encourage diversity of thought: Actively seek out team members with different backgrounds, experiences, and perspectives. Encourage them to share their unique viewpoints and challenge the status quo.

Create a safe space for dissent: Create an environment where team members feel comfortable expressing disagreement or alternative ideas without fear of reprisal. Encourage respectful debate and constructive criticism.

Assign the role of "devil's advocate": Designate a team member to purposely challenge the group's assumptions, play out worst-case scenarios, and present alternative viewpoints to stimulate critical thinking.

Avoid stating preferences upfront: As a leader, refrain from expressing your own opinions or preferences at the beginning of a discussion to prevent undue influence on the group's decision-making process.

Encourage independent thinking: Promote a culture where team members are expected to critically evaluate information and form their own opinions before engaging in group discussions.

Seek outside opinions: Invite external experts or stakeholders to provide their insights and challenge the group's assumptions. This can help break the cycle of insular thinking.

Ask the question "Why is this a bad idea?": Encourage team members to critically examine ideas and decisions by asking them to identify potential flaws, risks, or negative consequences. This simple question can help teams break free from the trap of groupthink and consider alternative perspectives. As a leader, you can model this behaviour by regularly asking your team, "We think this is a great idea, but let's take a moment to consider why it might be a bad idea." This approach supports a culture of critical thinking and helps teams identify potential pitfalls before making decisions. By implementing these strategies and regularly asking the question "Why is this a bad idea?", leaders can create a more inclusive and diverse decision-making process that mitigates the risks of groupthink and builds team resilience.

As Allegra Chapman mentioned in her podcast interview, "Disagreement can be positive, but it's how you handle it and it's how you create an environment where those sorts of potentially quite challenging conversations can happen in a respectful, positive, productive way."

Building a diverse and inclusive team

As we have explored throughout this chapter, the power of diversity in creating resilient teams cannot be overstated. Diverse teams bring a wealth of perspectives, experiences, and ideas to the table, enabling them to navigate challenges more effectively, adapt to change, and drive innovation. However, building a truly diverse and inclusive team requires intentional effort and commitment from leaders. So, how can you, as a leader, go about creating a team that harnesses the strength of diversity to create resilience?

Start with self-reflection and awareness

Before embarking on the journey of building a diverse and inclusive team, it's important to examine your own biases, assumptions, and leadership practices. Engage in honest self-reflection and seek feedback from others to identify areas where you can grow and improve as an inclusive leader. Cultivate a deep understanding of your privilege and how it may impact your decision-making and interactions with team members. This involves setting aside dedicated time to reflect on personal background, social identities, leadership practices, and decision-making processes, as well as seeking feedback from others. By identifying areas for growth and development, committing to ongoing learning and self-awareness, and integrating these insights into daily leadership practices, leaders can create a more inclusive team environment and become more effective in amplifying diverse voices. Sharing this journey of self-reflection and growth with others can also encourage a culture of continuous improvement and inclusivity within the organisation.

Set clear diversity and inclusion goals

While setting diversity and inclusion goals can be a delicate task, leaders must establish clear intentions and objectives. One effective approach is to develop specific, measurable, and time-bound goals that align with your organisation's overall strategy and values. These goals should take into account various factors, such as demographic representation, the incorporation of diverse perspectives, and the creation of an inclusive team culture. When crafting these goals, it is essential to communicate them clearly to your team and relevant stakeholders, ensuring that everyone understands their significance and the role they play in achieving them. Moreover, leaders must hold themselves and others accountable for progress, regularly monitoring and assessing the impact of their diversity and inclusion initiatives. By setting well-defined goals and creating a sense of shared responsibility, leaders can create a roadmap for building a more diverse and inclusive team while mitigating the risks associated with goal-setting in this sensitive area. And remember this is not about tick boxes and tokenism, it's about creating a diverse team that will be resilient due to the diversity.

Revamp your recruitment practices

To build a diverse and inclusive team, it is essential to critically examine and revamp your current recruitment practices. Begin by assessing your existing processes and identifying areas where bias may be present or where there are opportunities to attract a more diverse pool of candidates.

One key aspect to consider is the language used in your job descriptions. Ensure that your job postings focus on the essential skills and qualifications required for the role, rather than including unnecessary requirements that may inadvertently exclude certain groups. Additionally, be mindful of using gender-neutral language and avoiding words or phrases that may be perceived as biased towards a particular gender or group. To reach a wider range of qualified candidates, it is crucial to expand your recruitment channels beyond traditional methods. Actively seek out and partner with professional networks, community organisations, and educational institutions that cater to underrepresented communities. Attend diversity-focused job fairs and engage with diverse talent through targeted outreach programs. By casting a wider net, you increase the likelihood of attracting a more diverse applicant pool.

Another effective strategy to reduce unconscious bias in the initial screening process is to implement blind resume reviews. This involves removing personal identifiers such as names, ages, and educational institutions from resumes before they are evaluated by the hiring team. By focusing solely on the candidates' qualifications and experience, you can minimise the impact of unconscious biases related to factors such as race, gender, or socioeconomic background. When it comes to the interview stage, ensuring diverse representation on the interview panel is crucial. Strive to include individuals from different backgrounds, departments, and levels within the organisation. This diversity of perspectives can help to mitigate individual biases and provide a more well-rounded assessment of each candidate. Additionally, provide training to all interviewers on inclusive interviewing practices, such as asking consistent questions, avoiding assumptions, and focusing on job-related criteria.

In my experience as a leader, I have often found myself grappling with the concept of "cultural fit" when hiring new team members. It's a phrase that gets thrown around frequently, to ensure that the person we bring on board will seamlessly integrate into the existing team and organisational dynamics. However, upon deeper reflection, I have come to realise that prioritising "cultural fit" can work against our goals of building a diverse and inclusive team. When we place too much emphasis on finding someone who fits into our current culture, we risk perpetuating homogeneity and stifling the very diversity of thought and perspectives that we should be seeking. By focusing on "cultural fit," we may inadvertently exclude candidates who bring unique experiences, backgrounds, and ideas to the table, simply because they don't conform to our preconceived notions of what "fits" within our team.

Instead of striving for a "cultural fit," we should shift our focus to identifying individuals who align with our organisation's vision and values, and who possess the necessary skills and competencies to excel in the role. By prioritising alignment over fit, we open ourselves up to a broader pool of talent and create opportunities for fresh perspectives and innovative thinking to flourish within our team. When assessing potential hires, we should ask ourselves questions like: Does this person understand and believe in our organisation's mission? Do they embody the core values that guide our work? Can they bring the skills, knowledge, and expertise needed to drive our projects forward? By focusing on these fundamental aspects, we can build a team that is united by a shared sense of purpose and equipped with the diverse talents needed to tackle complex challenges.

Actively seeking out candidates with diverse lived experiences and unique perspectives contributes to the creation of a vibrant and multifaceted team. The rich tapestry of ideas and approaches forms the foundation for more innovative problem-solving and resilient outcomes. By intentionally bringing together individuals from different backgrounds, we tap into a wellspring of creativity and adaptability that strengthens the team's ability to navigate challenges. In my experience working with various boards, particularly those in the charitable sector, I have observed a growing recognition of the value of diversity and lived experience. These organisations are increasingly prioritising the recruitment of trustees who bring firsthand knowledge and understanding of the needs and challenges faced by the clients they serve. By actively seeking out individuals with lived experience, these boards aim to ensure that diverse perspectives are not only represented but also deeply understood and integrated into decision-making processes.

The inclusion of trustees with lived experience adds a layer of authenticity and depth to the board's understanding of the issues at hand. These individuals can provide valuable insights into the day-to-day realities faced by the organisation's beneficiaries, shedding light on the nuances and complexities that may not be apparent to those without direct experience. This deeper understanding enables the board to make more informed decisions, develop more targeted strategies, and ultimately, better serve the needs of their clients. Moreover, the presence of trustees with lived experience sends a powerful message about the organisation's commitment to diversity, inclusion, and representation. It demonstrates that the board values the voices and perspectives of those they serve and is willing to take concrete steps to ensure that these voices are heard and considered at the highest levels of decision-making. This commitment to diversity and inclusion not only strengthens the board's ability to make resilient decisions but also enhances the organisation's credibility and trust within the communities it serves. By actively seeking out and embracing the lived experiences and diverse perspectives of trustees, boards can tap into a rich source of knowledge, insights, and creativity. This diversity of thought and experience contributes to more robust problem-solving, more responsive strategies, and ultimately, more resilient outcomes that better serve the needs of the organisation's clients and stakeholders.

As leaders, it is our responsibility to cultivate a hiring process that values diversity, inclusion, and alignment with our organisational goals. This means being intentional about the language we use in job descriptions, the channels we use to reach potential candidates, and the criteria we prioritise when making hiring decisions. It also means creating an inclusive interview process that allows candidates to showcase their strengths and potential, rather than simply assessing their "fit" with our existing culture. Ultimately, by shifting our focus from "cultural fit" to alignment with our vision and values, we can build teams that are not only diverse in their composition but also united in their purpose. These are the teams that are best equipped to weather the storms of change, to innovate in the face of adversity, and to deliver meaningful impact in an ever-evolving world. As leaders, it is up to us to champion this shift in mindset and to create the conditions for diverse, inclusive, and resilient teams to thrive.

By implementing these strategies – crafting inclusive job descriptions, expanding recruitment channels, using blind resume screening, and ensuring diverse interview panels – you can significantly reduce bias in your hiring processes and attract a more diverse range of qualified candidates. Remember that building a diverse and inclusive team requires ongoing effort and continuous improvement. Regularly assess and refine your hiring practices based on feedback and results to ensure that you are making progress towards your diversity and inclusion goals.

Foster an inclusive team culture

While building a diverse team is an important step towards developing resilience and innovation, it is only the beginning of the journey. Equally important is the creation of an inclusive culture that allows every team member to feel like their thoughts and perspectives are valued, respected, and able to be heard. As a leader, it is your responsibility to actively cultivate an environment where diversity can flourish and where every individual feels a deep sense of belonging and psychological safety.

To promote inclusivity, you must prioritise open communication and encourage team members to share their thoughts, experiences, and concerns freely. This means creating spaces and platforms where diverse voices can be heard and acknowledged, whether through regular team meetings, one-on-one conversations, or anonymous feedback channels. By actively listening to and valuing the insights of all team members, you demonstrate that their contributions matter and that their perspectives are integral to the team's success. Moreover, it is essential to move beyond simply tolerating diversity and instead actively celebrate and build on the unique strengths and experiences that each team member brings to the table. This involves creating opportunities for everyone to contribute meaningfully to projects, decision-making processes, and problem-solving efforts. By tapping into the diverse skill sets and knowledge bases within your team, you can create an environment of collaboration and innovation, where different ideas and approaches are not only welcomed but also encouraged.

However, building an inclusive culture also requires a proactive stance against any instances of bias, discrimination, or microaggressions that may arise within the team. As a leader, you must be vigilant in identifying and addressing these issues swiftly and effectively, demonstrating a zero-tolerance policy for exclusionary behaviour. This means having difficult conversations, holding individuals accountable for their actions, and taking steps to educate and raise awareness about the impact of bias and discrimination on team dynamics and performance. To support these efforts, it is important to provide ongoing training and development opportunities that promote diversity, equity, and inclusion within your team. This can include workshops on unconscious bias, cultural competency, and inclusive communication strategies, as well as mentorship programs that pair team members from different backgrounds to foster understanding and collaboration. By investing in the continuous growth and development of your team members, you create a culture of learning and self-awareness that is essential for building resilience and adaptability.

Furthermore, as a leader, you must model the inclusive behaviours and attitudes that you wish to see within your team. This means being mindful of your own biases and privileges, actively seeking out and amplifying diverse perspectives, and demonstrating a genuine commitment to creating an equitable and respectful work environment. By leading by example and consistently reinforcing the value of inclusivity through your words and actions, you set the tone for the entire team and create a shared sense of responsibility for building a culture of belonging. By prioritising inclusivity alongside diversity, you lay the foundation for a resilient and adaptive team that can navigate challenges, drive innovation, and achieve extraordinary results.

Remember, building a diverse and inclusive team is an ongoing journey, not a one-time initiative. It requires consistent effort, commitment, and a willingness to learn and grow as a leader. By prioritising diversity and inclusion, you not only create a more resilient team but also contribute to a more equitable and just workplace and society. Embrace the challenge, lead by example, and watch your team thrive in the face of adversity.

How about belonging?

In the context of team resilience, diversity, inclusion, and belonging play pivotal roles in creating a robust and adaptive team environment. Each element contributes uniquely to the team's ability to overcome challenges.

"Diversity is being invited to the party and inclusion is being asked to dance." This quote by Verna Myers, the former Global Head of Inclusion Strategy at Netflix, was shared by Chico Chakravorty, a leading figure in organisational culture enhancement, employee belonging improvement, and champion of Doing Diversity Differently. He shared this enlightening perspective during his appearance on my Helping Organisations Thrive podcast. This quote encapsulates the foundational principles of diversity and inclusion within a team. Diversity refers to the presence of individuals from various backgrounds, experiences, and perspectives. Inclusion is a choice we have to make to reap the benefits of diversity. It's about inviting different voices to the table and recognising the value that each person brings to the team. Diversity is not enough. Inclusion is the next step—it's about actively engaging and involving every team member in decision-making processes, discussions, and activities. Inclusion creates a sense of belonging and ensures that all team members feel valued and respected for their contributions.

Here's a profound insight from Chico Chakravorty that extends Verna Myers's quote and states: "Belonging is choosing the music on the playlist and bringing food to the buffet table." In essence, belonging extends beyond diversity and inclusion, developing an environment where each team member experiences a profound sense of connection, ownership, and empowerment. When team members feel like they belong, they are not just passive participants; they actively shape the team culture and dynamics. They have the autonomy to contribute ideas, express themselves authentically, be willing to go the extra mile and make meaningful contributions to team goals. Choosing the music on the playlist symbolises having a voice in shaping the team's direction and culture. Bringing food to the buffet table represents actively contributing to the team's collective success and well-being. More importantly, the extension of this quote moves the original statement from a place of having to be asked or invited (a position of passive action) to something which is far more active in its intention and behaviour.

In the context of team resilience, diversity, inclusion, and belonging are essential components that contribute to the team's ability to navigate challenges, adapt to change, and bounce back from setbacks. A diverse team brings a wealth of perspectives, experiences, and skills to the table, enabling it to approach problems from multiple angles and find innovative solutions. Inclusion ensures that every team member feels supported, heard, and valued, building a collaborative and supportive team culture. Belonging empowers team members to take ownership of their roles, collaborate effectively, and work towards common goals with a shared sense of purpose and commitment. Incorporating these principles of diversity, inclusion, and belonging into your team resilience strategy can enhance the team's ability to withstand adversity, encourage innovation, and achieve greater success in today's rapidly changing and diverse work environments.

Chapter summary

In this chapter, we explored the critical role of diversity in building resilient teams. Drawing from personal experiences and research-backed insights, we explored the multifaceted benefits of diversity, including encouraging innovation, adaptability, psychological safety, and customer understanding. We also examined the importance of neurodiversity and how embracing different ways of thinking and problem-solving can strengthen a team's resilience. The chapter highlighted strategies for overcoming groupthink and building a diverse and inclusive team, such as self-reflection, setting clear goals, revamping recruitment practices, and fostering an inclusive culture. Ultimately, the chapter emphasises that building a diverse and inclusive team is an ongoing journey that requires consistent effort, commitment, and a willingness to learn and grow as a leader, but the rewards of enhanced resilience, innovation, and success make it a worthwhile endeavour.

Reflection

Reflect on a time when your team faced a significant challenge. How could diverse perspectives and thought processes have contributed to finding more effective solutions? Consider the potential benefits of having a team with varied backgrounds, experiences, and ways of thinking in such situations.

Examine your own biases, assumptions, and leadership practices. Identify areas where you can grow and improve as an inclusive leader. How can you cultivate a deeper understanding of your privilege and its impact on your decision-making and interactions with team members?

Evaluate your current team composition and recruitment practices. Are there opportunities to attract a more diverse pool of candidates? Consider how you can revamp job descriptions, expand recruitment channels, and implement blind resume reviews to reduce bias and support diversity.

Reflect on the level of psychological safety and inclusion within your team. Do all team members feel valued, respected, and empowered to contribute their unique perspectives? What steps can you take to create an environment where everyone feels a sense of belonging and can bring their authentic selves to work?

Consider the role of neurodiversity in building resilient teams. How can you foster an environment that values and leverages the unique strengths and perspectives of neurodivergent individuals? Reflect on the potential benefits of creating an inclusive culture that supports and empowers neurodiverse team members.

Action

Conduct a diversity audit of your current team composition. Analyse demographic data, identify gaps in representation, and assess how well your team reflects the diversity of your industry, community, and customer base. Use this information to set specific, measurable goals for improving diversity and inclusion within your team.

Revamp your recruitment practices to attract a more diverse pool of candidates. Review job descriptions for biased language, expand your recruitment channels to reach underrepresented communities, implement blind resume screening, and ensure diverse representation on interview panels. Provide training for interviewers on inclusive hiring practices and mitigating unconscious bias.

Create an inclusive team culture by prioritising open communication, psychological safety, and a sense of belonging. Create regular opportunities for team members to share their thoughts, experiences, and concerns through team meetings, one-on-one conversations, and anonymous feedback channels. Celebrate the unique strengths and contributions of each team member and actively promote a culture of collaboration and mutual respect.

Educate yourself and your team on diversity, inclusion, and unconscious bias. Invest in ongoing training and development opportunities, such as workshops on cultural competency, inclusive communication, and mitigating bias. Encourage team members to engage in self-reflection and share their insights and experiences to encourage a culture of continuous learning and growth.

Embrace neurodiversity by creating an inclusive environment that supports and values the unique perspectives and strengths of neurodivergent individuals. Provide accommodations such as flexible work arrangements, quiet spaces, and clear communication channels. Develop a culture that celebrates differences and encourages open dialogue about neurodiversity.

PART FOUR
EMBRACING ADAPTABILITY IN THE FUTURE OF WORK

CHAPTER SEVEN: CREATING HYBRID/REMOTE RESILIENT TEAMS

What you will gain from this chapter

Insights into the unique challenges and opportunities that remote and hybrid work presents for building and sustaining team resilience.

An understanding of the five key principles essential for creating resilience in remote and hybrid teams: connectivity, belonging, communication, visibility, and well-being support.

Practical strategies and real-world examples to help leaders and teams adapt to the evolving nature of work, leverage technology effectively, and create a supportive and inclusive team culture.

Knowledge of how to maintain connectivity among team members, and develop strong interpersonal relationships and trust in a remote setting.

Techniques for cultivating a sense of belonging within remote and hybrid teams, including establishing a shared identity and purpose, and creating opportunities for social connection.

Best practices for effective communication in remote and hybrid environments, promoting open dialogue, active listening, and transparency.

Insights into the importance of well-being support in building resilient teams, and strategies for prioritising mental health, self-care, and work-life balance in a remote work context.

Insight: Navigating the changing future of work

For an entire year, I coached the rowing team without ever meeting them face-to-face. Our interactions were confined to virtual screens, a situation increasingly familiar in today's remote and hybrid work environments. As many of you navigate similar circumstances, making connections with colleagues you may never encounter in person, the significance of adapting to this new norm becomes apparent. The experience of coaching the rowing team remotely was a testament to the changing landscape of work and collaboration. In the past, in-person meetings and face-to-face interactions were the default mode of engagement. However, the rapid adoption of remote and hybrid work models has challenged traditional notions of teamwork and relationship-building. The rowing team and I found ourselves navigating this new reality, discovering ways to create connection, trust, and resilience through our screens. Throughout this remote coaching journey, we used various digital platforms and tools to facilitate our interactions. Regular video conferences became our virtual meeting grounds, allowing us to see each other's faces, share ideas, and provide support. However, building relationships and establishing trust in a remote setting presented its own set of challenges. Without the benefit of in-person interactions, we had to be intentional in creating opportunities for connection and rapport. We dedicated time to team-building activities and informal check-ins. These moments of casual interaction helped to break down barriers, foster a sense of camaraderie, and create a supportive team environment.

Interestingly, even when given the option for in-person coaching, several of my one-on-one coaching clients preferred to continue with online sessions. This preference highlights the growing acceptance and comfort of remote interactions. People are recognising the benefits of flexibility, convenience, and the ability to connect with others regardless of geographic location. The virtual coaching experience has opened up new possibilities for individuals to access support and guidance from the comfort of their own spaces. As we navigate this new world of work, we must acknowledge that remote and hybrid arrangements are here to stay. The pandemic has accelerated the adoption of these models, and many organisations are embracing the benefits of flexibility and remote collaboration. However, this shift requires a proactive approach to building and sustaining resilient teams. Leaders and team members alike must adapt to the unique challenges and opportunities presented by remote and hybrid work.

Building resilience in a remote or hybrid setting involves intentionally fostering connection, communication, and trust among team members. It requires leveraging technology effectively, establishing clear expectations, and creating a supportive and inclusive team culture. Leaders must be proactive in providing the necessary resources and support to enable their teams to thrive in this new reality. As we move forward, it is essential to embrace the evolving nature of work and be open to new ways of collaboration and relationship-building. The story of coaching the rowing team remotely serves as a reminder that resilience can be cultivated even in the most unconventional circumstances. By adapting to change, leveraging technology, and prioritising human connection, we can build strong, resilient teams that can navigate the challenges and opportunities of the remote and hybrid work landscape.

What are the challenges to building team resilience in a hybrid/remote world?

One of the primary challenges is maintaining connectivity among team members. In a remote setting, the lack of face-to-face interactions can hinder the development of strong interpersonal relationships and trust. Without the spontaneous conversations and informal exchanges that occur in a shared physical space, team members may feel disconnected from one another. This lack of connectivity can impact team cohesion, collaboration, and overall resilience. To overcome this challenge, teams must prioritise regular virtual team-building activities, encourage open communication channels, and use technology to facilitate seamless collaboration.

Another significant challenge is creating a sense of belonging within remote and hybrid teams. When team members work from different locations, they may feel isolated and detached from the larger organisational culture. The absence of shared experiences and informal social interactions can impact team morale and engagement. A recent study by Deloitte found that 47% of remote workers reported feeling less connected to their colleagues, and 42% felt less connected to their organisation (Deloitte, 2022). To address this challenge, teams must actively cultivate an inclusive and supportive team culture. This can be achieved by regularly recognising individual contributions, celebrating team successes, and creating opportunities for social connection and informal interactions.

Effective communication is also a critical challenge in remote and hybrid work environments. Without the benefit of face-to-face interactions and nonverbal cues, misunderstandings and miscommunications can arise more easily. A survey by Gartner revealed that 52% of remote workers experienced communication challenges, and 44% faced difficulties in collaborating effectively (Gartner, 2022). To overcome this challenge, teams must establish clear communication protocols, use technology for effective information sharing, and prioritise regular check-ins and feedback loops. Leaders should also actively promote open dialogue, encourage active listening, and promote a culture of transparency and trust.

Maintaining visibility and accountability can be challenging in remote and hybrid teams. When team members work independently from different locations, tracking progress, ensuring alignment, and providing timely support can be difficult. A study by PwC found that 38% of remote workers felt less visible to their managers, and 31% believed that their contributions were not fully recognised (PwC, 2022). To address this challenge, teams must establish clear goals and expectations, implement regular performance check-ins, and leverage technology for transparent progress tracking. Leaders should also actively seek opportunities to showcase team successes, provide visible support and resources, and establish a culture of accountability and recognition.

In the rapidly evolving landscape of remote and hybrid work, teams face unique challenges that can impact their resilience and overall effectiveness. A recent study by McKinsey & Company found that 49% of remote workers reported feeling fatigued and stressed, while 37% struggled with maintaining work-life balance (McKinsey, 2022). Additionally, a survey by Microsoft revealed that 54% of remote workers felt overworked, and 39% experienced burnout (Microsoft, 2022). These findings highlight the growing importance of addressing the well-being challenges associated with remote and hybrid work environments. Well-being support has emerged as a critical principle in building resilient remote and hybrid teams. The challenges of remote work, such as isolation, burnout, and blurred work-life boundaries, can significantly impact the mental health and well-being of team members. A survey by Oracle found that 78% of remote workers reported increased stress levels, and 76% experienced heightened anxiety (Oracle, 2022). To address this challenge, organisations must prioritise the well-being of their remote and hybrid teams. This can be achieved by implementing flexible work arrangements, providing access to mental health resources, encouraging regular breaks and time off, and building a culture of empathy and support. Leaders should also engage in open conversations about well-being, promote healthy work habits, and lead by example in prioritising self-care.

By actively addressing these challenges and prioritising the five key principles of connectivity, belonging, communication, visibility, and well-being support, teams can build and sustain resilience in the remote and hybrid work landscape. Through intentional efforts to develop strong interpersonal relationships, create an inclusive team culture, establish effective communication channels, maintain transparency and accountability, and prioritise the well-being of team members, organisations can overcome the unique challenges posed by remote and hybrid work and thrive in the face of adversity.

The first principle is connectivity

In the era of hybrid and remote work, connectivity has emerged as a critical factor in building and sustaining team resilience. Connectivity goes beyond mere technological links; it encompasses the emotional bonds, interpersonal relationships, and sense of unity that bind team members together, regardless of their physical location. When teams are connected, they form a resilient network.

In a remote or hybrid setting, creating connectivity requires intentional effort and strategic initiatives. Ensure that as a leader you have the intention to have connectivity within your teams and organisation. Without the natural opportunities for impromptu interactions and face-to-face communication, teams must actively create spaces and opportunities for connection. Regular virtual team-building activities, such as online coffee breaks, shared learning sessions, or even virtual escape rooms, can help team members bond and develop a sense of camaraderie. These activities provide a platform for individuals to interact on a personal level, share experiences, and build trust, which are essential components of a resilient team.

During the pandemic, I had a thought-provoking discussion with the CEO of a large organisation about maintaining connectivity in a remote setting. Before the pandemic, this CEO had an open-door policy, welcoming employees at all levels to drop by his office for a chat. However, with the shift to remote work, he faced the challenge of preserving this culture of accessibility and openness. To address this, the CEO came up with an innovative solution. He decided to send his personal Zoom link to all 200 employees in the organisation. Throughout the workday, from start to finish, he kept his Zoom meeting room open. This virtual open-door policy allowed employees to enter the Zoom waiting room whenever they wanted to have a conversation with him. During breaks between meetings, the CEO would check the waiting room and invite individuals in for a chat. These conversations could last anywhere from a minute to a more extended discussion, depending on the situation. Of course, when the CEO was engaged in formal meetings, he would not admit anyone from the waiting room, but employees understood and respected this boundary. This approach effectively recreated the open office culture in a virtual setting. Through his use of Zoom, the CEO showed his availability and approachability, demonstrating his dedication to keeping lines of communication open and encouraging a sense of connectedness with his staff. I believe this is a fantastic idea that other leaders can adapt to their own remote or hybrid teams. One suggestion would be to establish dedicated time slots as to when the virtual door is open, ensuring that employees know when they can drop in for a chat. For example, a leader could set aside an hour or two each day, perhaps in the morning or afternoon, when their Zoom link is open for impromptu conversations. By implementing such practices, leaders can create a virtual environment that promotes connectivity, accessibility, and a sense of belonging among team members. This open and approachable leadership style can contribute significantly to building trust, supporting collaboration, and strengthening the overall resilience of the team, even in a remote or hybrid setting.

Building upon the open-door policy approach via Zoom, one of the key strategies for enhancing connectivity is to prioritise open and transparent communication. Leaders should establish clear communication channels and encourage team members to share their thoughts, ideas, and concerns openly. Regular check-ins, both one-on-one and as a team, provide opportunities for individuals to express themselves, seek support, and feel heard. By creating a safe and inclusive environment where everyone's voice is valued, teams can create a sense of belonging and strengthen their emotional connection. Technology plays a vital role in facilitating connectivity in hybrid and remote teams. The use of collaboration tools, such as video conferencing platforms, instant messaging apps, and project management software, can help bridge the gap between dispersed team members. These tools enable effective communication, real-time collaboration, and the ability to share information and resources effortlessly. By providing teams with the right technological infrastructure and training them on how to use these tools effectively, organisations can create a connected and resilient workforce.

Informal social interactions are equally important in building connectivity and resilience. Encouraging virtual water cooler conversations, organising online social events, or even creating dedicated channels for non-work-related discussions can help team members connect on a personal level. These informal interactions create a sense of community and provide opportunities for team members to share their experiences, challenges, and successes, creating a supportive and empathetic environment. For example, another conversation I had with a leader of a global organisation implemented a weekly "Virtual Coffee and Connect" session, where team members were randomly paired for a 15-minute informal video call. These sessions provided an opportunity for team members to get to know each other beyond their work roles, share personal stories, and build genuine connections. As a result, the team reported increased trust, collaboration, and resilience, even in the face of tight deadlines and challenging projects. Another approach and building upon the "Virtual Coffee and Connect" is to implement a "Virtual Buddy System," where team members are paired up and encouraged to have regular informal check-ins. These connections not only will help team members feel less isolated but also foster a sense of accountability and support. If a team member faces a personal challenge, their buddy can be there to offer encouragement and assistance, demonstrating the resilience and strength of our connected team.

Another powerful strategy for promoting connectivity is to celebrate successes and milestones together. Recognising individual and team achievements, both big and small, helps develop a sense of pride and belonging. Team members might bond over virtual events like online award ceremonies or shared virtual experiences, which help to strengthen their sense of unity. By acknowledging and celebrating the contributions of each team member, leaders can develop a culture of appreciation and support, which is essential for building resilience.

Ultimately, connectivity is the lifeblood of resilient hybrid and remote teams. By prioritising open communication, leveraging technology, encouraging informal interactions, celebrating successes, and creating opportunities for personal connections, teams can build a strong foundation of trust, support, and unity. When teams are connected, they are better equipped to navigate challenges, adapt to change, and emerge stronger together.

The second principle is belonging

Belonging goes beyond mere inclusion; it is the feeling of being accepted, valued, and connected to one's team and organisation. When team members feel a strong sense of belonging, they are more likely to be engaged, motivated, and committed to their work, even in the face of challenges and uncertainties. Creating a sense of belonging in a hybrid or remote setting requires deliberate effort and focused strategies. One powerful approach is to establish a shared team identity and purpose. By clearly articulating the team's mission, values, and goals, leaders can help team members understand how their efforts contribute to the broader organisational objectives. This alignment creates a sense of unity and belonging, as everyone recognises their role in achieving a common purpose.

Recently, I had the opportunity to work with a client's senior leadership team on clarifying their organisation's overall vision and values. This is a process I thoroughly enjoy undertaking with organisations, as it lays the foundation for a strong sense of belonging and shared direction. Throughout the visioning and values clarification process, I placed great emphasis on ensuring that every individual in the room had the opportunity to contribute and be heard. By actively soliciting input from all team members and valuing their perspectives, we created an inclusive environment where everyone felt that their opinions mattered. During the sessions, I facilitated discussions and exercises that encouraged open dialogue and collaborative problem-solving. We explored questions such as, "What do we stand for as an organisation?" and "How can we create a culture where everyone feels valued and connected?" By engaging in these conversations, the leadership team gained a deeper understanding of each other's viewpoints and developed a shared sense of purpose. As we progressed through the process, I observed a palpable shift in the team's dynamics. Team members who had previously been hesitant to speak up began to actively participate, sharing their insights and ideas. The atmosphere in the room transformed from one of individual contributions to a collective sense of ownership and belonging. By the end of the visioning and values clarification process, the senior leadership team had not only developed a clear and compelling vision for their organisation but also forged a stronger bond as a team. They recognised that their contributions were essential to the success of the whole organisation, and they felt a deep sense of belonging to both the process and the organisation. This experience reinforced my belief in the power of inclusive leadership and the importance of creating opportunities for everyone to contribute meaningfully. When team members feel that their voices are heard and their contributions are valued, they are more likely to develop a strong sense of belonging, even in a hybrid or remote setting.

Regular team meetings and discussions that reinforce the shared identity and vision are vital for creating unity and belonging in physically dispersed teams. These gatherings, whether virtual town halls, team huddles, or informal coffee chats, provide opportunities for team members to connect, align, and celebrate their collective purpose. During these meetings, leaders should prioritise discussions around the team's mission, values, and goals, consistently reiterating and reinforcing the shared identity. This helps team members maintain a clear sense of purpose and direction, even when working remotely. These meetings also serve as a forum for sharing updates, successes, and challenges, encouraging transparency, collaboration, and a shared sense of accountability. By openly discussing progress, celebrating achievements, and addressing obstacles together, team members develop stronger bonds and camaraderie. Moreover, allocating time for personal stories, experiences, or virtual team-building activities during these meetings helps break down barriers, build trust, and create a sense of connection, even when team members are not physically together. By consistently emphasising the team's purpose, encouraging collaboration, and providing opportunities for personal connection through regular meetings and discussions, leaders can create a strong sense of unity and belonging in hybrid and remote teams.

Recognition and appreciation are powerful tools for promoting belonging. Regularly acknowledging and celebrating the contributions and achievements of team members, both individually and collectively, can make them feel valued and connected to the team. Leaders can implement peer recognition programs, where team members can nominate and celebrate each other's successes, encouraging a culture of gratitude and support.

I had the pleasure of interviewing Jonathan Fields the Co-Founder and CEO of Assembly on my podcast (Helping Organisations Thrive), where he shared, "It's a fundamental aspect of human nature to desire acknowledgement for one's efforts. Before founding this company, I came across an article by Gallup, a well-established survey company. They conducted an extensive survey involving 25,000 employees across a vast array of companies. The findings were striking: less than one-third of those employees had received recognition in the past two weeks. Moreover, the same proportion reported that their most recent instance of going above and beyond went unnoticed. Let's set aside the statistics for a moment and consider this from a common-sense perspective. Imagine yourself as a mid-level employee at a company, pouring your heart and soul into your work, and doing everything in your power to achieve success. You deliver exceptional results, but your efforts go completely unacknowledged. How would that make you feel? Would it inspire you to continue striving for excellence? The answer is clear: of course not. When our contributions are recognised and appreciated, it ignites a powerful motivation within us. We are driven to work harder, to continue excelling, and to repeatedly go the extra mile. This fundamental truth lies at the core of why we established our company, Assembly. We understand the profound impact that recognition and acknowledgement can have on employee engagement, productivity, and overall job satisfaction." Jonathan's company Assembly helps organisations with engagement, and connection along with rewards and recognition, and this is especially good for those who work remotely/hybrid.

Another way to foster a strong sense of belonging is to start each virtual team meeting with a "belonging check-in," where team members share one thing that made them feel connected to the team that week. This simple practice can help you build trust, empathy, and understanding, even when you are working remotely. By making this a regular practice, you create an opportunity for team members to actively think about and appreciate the moments that contribute to their sense of belonging. It also allows the team to collectively celebrate and reinforce the positive experiences that strengthen their bond. Moreover, the "belonging check-in" encourages a culture of empathy and understanding within the team. As team members share their experiences, they gain insights into each other's perspectives and challenges. This heightened awareness and appreciation of one another's experiences can lead to increased trust, support, and collaboration.

In conclusion, a sense of belonging is the foundation of resilient hybrid and remote teams. By establishing a shared identity, creating an inclusive environment, providing opportunities for social connection, recognising contributions, and supporting employee resource groups, leaders can cultivate a strong sense of belonging. When team members feel accepted, valued, and connected, they are better equipped to navigate challenges, adapt to change, and thrive together, even in the most demanding circumstances.

The third principle is communication

Communication goes beyond the mere exchange of information; it is the foundation upon which trust, collaboration, and shared understanding are built. When teams are dispersed across different locations and time zones, clear, consistent, and empathetic communication becomes the glue that holds them together, enabling them to navigate challenges and thrive during challenging times.

Establishing clear communication channels and protocols is essential for hybrid and remote teams. This involves identifying the most appropriate tools and platforms for different types of communication, such as video conferencing for team meetings, instant messaging for quick updates, and project management software for collaborative work. By ensuring that everyone is on the same page regarding how and when to communicate, teams can minimise misunderstandings and maintain a smooth flow of information. When I spoke with Jonathan Fields on my podcast he noted the following regarding effective communication, "Zoom fatigue is a real thing, don't get me wrong. But if you can chat with someone like I'm looking at you right now, you can see emotions, you can understand better. Although you lose certain aspects of engagement, for example, you can't tell right now if my legs or hands are fidgeting, but you can get closer to face-to-face engagement if you're on video. Therefore, I recommend important meetings be on video. Don't do it by text, don't do it by Slack. At Assembly we do a really interesting thing: daily updates. Transparency is key. I want to know what people are doing. I want them to know what I'm doing. Every morning we encourage a short 2-minute blurb, answering questions as simple as "Hey, what are you doing?" "What is your plan today?" "Are there any obstacles, or anything we can help you with?" Personally, I love it. I know what everybody's doing. It's tangible." Regular check-ins and team meetings are essential for maintaining alignment and connection. Leaders should encourage open dialogue, active listening, and constructive feedback during these meetings. To address the lack of nonverbal cues in remote communication, teams should use video conferencing to simulate face-to-face interactions, encouraging the use of cameras to help team members feel more connected and engaged.

Setting aside dedicated time for informal communication and team-building activities is an effective strategy for developing a strong sense of belonging within your team. By introducing virtual coffee breaks, casual check-ins, or online gaming sessions as shared in the connectivity section, leaders create opportunities for team members to connect on a personal level and engage in light-hearted conversations. In a hybrid working environment, it's essential to acknowledge that asking for help might feel less natural for some team members, as my daughter pointed out from her own experience. She mentioned that "it feels less natural asking someone a quick 'help' question" when working remotely. As a leader, it's crucial to recognise this challenge and consider how you can create an environment that encourages your team to seek assistance when needed, regardless of their physical location. Creating open communication channels, scheduling regular check-ins, encouraging a supportive team culture, and providing resources and training are all effective ways to address this issue. By prioritising these aspects of your leadership approach, you can help your team feel more comfortable reaching out for support, even in a hybrid setting. Ultimately, this will lead to a more collaborative, productive, and satisfied team, despite the challenges that come with working in a hybrid environment. These informal moments help break down barriers, encourage empathy, and create a more human-centred work environment. They contribute to a culture of trust, psychological safety, and mutual support, where team members feel comfortable being themselves and relying on one another.

And finally, in my experience, one of the most powerful ways to build resilience through communication is by leading with empathy and transparency. During my time coaching the rowing team, I made it a point to check in with each team member individually, listening to their concerns and offering support. By being open about the challenges we were facing and the steps we were taking to address them, I was able to build trust and maintain morale. Ultimately, effective communication is key to building resilient hybrid and remote teams. By establishing clear channels, promoting open dialogue, leveraging technology, and leading with empathy and transparency, leaders can create a strong foundation for collaboration, trust, and resilience. When teams communicate effectively, they are better equipped to navigate challenges, adapt to change, and emerge stronger together.

The fourth principle is visibility

Visibility goes beyond mere presence; it encompasses the ability to be seen, heard, and recognised for one's contributions, regardless of physical location. When team members feel visible, they are more likely to be engaged, motivated, and connected to their work and their colleagues, creating a sense of belonging and purpose that is essential for resilience.

One of the key challenges of remote work is the potential for team members to feel isolated and disconnected from their colleagues and the broader organisation. Without the informal interactions and spontaneous conversations that occur naturally in a shared physical space, it can be easy for individuals to feel like they are working in a vacuum. This lack of visibility can lead to feelings of loneliness, disengagement, and even burnout, undermining the resilience of both individuals and the team as a whole. To promote visibility in hybrid and remote teams, leaders must be intentional and proactive in their approach. There are several strategies already shared in this chapter which include regular check-ins and one-on-one meetings with team members. These meetings provide an opportunity for individuals to share updates on their work, discuss challenges and successes, and receive feedback and support from their managers. By carving out dedicated time for these conversations, leaders can ensure that every team member feels seen and heard, even when working remotely. And as already shared, leveraging technology to create virtual spaces for collaboration and connection is invaluable. Tools like video conferencing, instant messaging, and project management software can help team members stay connected and engaged, even when working from different locations. By encouraging the use of these tools for both formal meetings and informal conversations, leaders can create a sense of visibility and belonging among team members.

During a conversation with a leader of a remote team during the pandemic, I learned about a powerful example of how visibility can contribute to team resilience. As the world shifted to remote work overnight, many of their team members struggled with feelings of isolation and disconnection. To combat this, they implemented a daily stand-up meeting via Zoom, where each team member had the opportunity to share their current work, challenges, and support needs. Additionally, they created a virtual "watercooler" channel on their instant messaging platform, allowing team members to share personal updates, photos, and stories. While I understand that during the pandemic, there was a sense of managing panic within teams, and a daily stand-up meeting might be too frequent, the underlying principle remains valid, along with the concept of a "watercooler" channel. These simple practices had a profound impact on the visibility and resilience of their team. By creating regular opportunities for connection and sharing, they were able to maintain a sense of cohesion and support, even as they navigated the challenges of remote work. Moreover, by publicly celebrating the successes and milestones of their team members, they fostered a culture of appreciation and recognition that kept everyone engaged and motivated.

Ultimately, visibility is one of the keys to unlocking the resilience of hybrid and remote teams. By being intentional and proactive in promoting visibility, leaders can create a culture of connection, support, and appreciation that enables teams to thrive. Whether through regular check-ins, virtual collaboration spaces, or public recognition, the power of visibility cannot be underestimated in building and sustaining resilient teams.

The fifth principle is well-being support

Well-being support goes beyond mere physical health; it encompasses the emotional, mental, and social aspects of an individual's overall well-being. When team members feel supported, cared for, and empowered to prioritise their well-being, they are more likely to be resilient, engaged, and productive, even in the face of challenges and uncertainty. The shift to remote work has blurred the lines between work and personal life, leading to increased stress, anxiety, and burnout among many employees. The lack of physical separation between work and home, coupled with the challenges of social isolation and virtual communication, can take a toll on an individual's well-being. As a result, leaders need to prioritise well-being support as a key component of their team's resilience strategy.

One effective approach to promoting well-being in hybrid and remote teams is to encourage open conversations about mental health and self-care. Leaders can create a safe and supportive environment where team members feel comfortable sharing their struggles and seeking help when needed. This can be achieved through regular check-ins, one-on-one conversations, and team discussions that normalise talking about well-being and mental health.

Another key strategy is to provide resources and support for self-care and stress management. This can include offering access to employee assistance programs, mental health services, and wellness resources such as meditation apps or virtual fitness classes. Leaders can also encourage team members to take regular breaks, disconnect from work outside of business hours, and prioritise activities that promote physical and emotional well-being.

In a recent interview on the "Helping Organisation Thrive" podcast with Tarin Calmeyer, the founder of RemoteTeamWellness.com, several strategies were discussed to support wellness in remote organisations. Tarin shared several insightful strategies that can help support your team's well-being.

Maintain social connections: Tarin emphasises the importance of reaching out to people, sending messages, joining support groups, or engaging in activities that fulfil your need for social connection and engagement. She states, "Socially, we all need to keep those connections up. And that may mean you have to reach out to people. That may mean that you have to make an effort to send a message or join a support group or join something that you are feeding your need for social connection and your need for social engagement."

Set boundaries with technology

Tarin recommends taking time away from screens, notifications, alerts, and media news. She suggests setting boundaries, such as not checking your phone first thing in the morning and instead taking a few moments to ground yourself with deep breaths or a walk. According to Tarin, "Time away from screens, is time away from all the constant onslaught of notifications, alerts, and media news. These are all things that are constantly trying to gain our attention, and are detrimental to our mental health."

Implement well-being practices in the workplace

Tarin advises organisations to show they care about individuals by sending out weekly wellness emails, well-being tips, or reminders to take breaks and move away from the screen. She also encourages mindful moments before meetings where everyone takes a breath together. In her words, "Whether it is something that may get sent out weekly, such as a weekly wellness email, or a weekly wellbeing tip, it is so easy to implement these things. For example, simply send a quick email suggesting a few at-desk stretches to encourage movement throughout the day. Maybe you send out a notification every single day at noon to encourage employees to get up and walk away from their screen for five minutes. Maybe it means setting a mindful moment right before your meetings where everyone just takes a breath together."

Make well-being a consistent practice

Tarin emphasises that well-being should be approached as "a practice, a daily routine. It's a lifelong journey. It's not just one and done." Tarin encourages individuals to incorporate small tools and practices into their daily lives, creating a domino effect of wellness. She also highlights the important role leaders play in modelling this behaviour by prioritising their well-being and demonstrating the importance of consistent self-care practices.

Building upon what Tarin shares, it is the role of a leader to facilitate such an approach to well-being. Leaders can set this example by:

Openly discussing their well-being practices and challenges.

Encouraging team members to take breaks and prioritise self-care.

Participating in company-wide wellness initiatives.

Sharing personal anecdotes about the benefits of consistent well-being practices.

Creating a culture that values and supports employee well-being.

By role modelling consistent well-being practices, leaders can inspire their teams to embrace wellness as a daily habit and create a supportive environment that encourages everyone to prioritise their physical, mental, and emotional health. By setting an example of self-care, boundary-setting, and work-life balance, leaders can create a culture that values and supports well-being at all levels of the organisation.

Ultimately, well-being support is foundational in building resilient hybrid and remote teams. By creating a culture that values and prioritises well-being, leaders can empower their teams to thrive, even in the face of adversity. Whether through open conversations, access to resources, or modelling healthy behaviours, the power of well-being support cannot be underestimated in building and sustaining resilient teams in the era of hybrid and remote work.

Chapter Summary

In this chapter, we explored the unique challenges and opportunities that remote and hybrid working presents for building and sustaining team resilience, focusing on the five key principles essential for building resilience: connectivity, belonging, communication, visibility, and well-being support. Drawing from personal experiences and insights from industry experts, the chapter provided actionable strategies and real-world examples to help leaders and teams adapt to the evolving nature of work, use technology effectively, establish clear expectations, and create a supportive and inclusive team culture. By prioritising these principles and addressing the specific challenges faced by remote and hybrid teams, leaders can build strong, resilient teams capable of navigating the uncertainties and complexities of the modern work landscape.

Reflection

Reflect on your experience working in a remote or hybrid setting. What challenges have you faced in maintaining connectivity, fostering a sense of belonging, and collaborating effectively with your team?

How can you, as a leader or team member, actively create opportunities for informal interactions, team-building activities, and personal connections in a virtual work environment?

Consider the communication channels and tools your team currently uses. How can you optimise these to enhance clarity, transparency, and inclusivity in your remote or hybrid team's communication?

Reflect on a time when you felt isolated or disconnected while working remotely. What strategies could you or your team implement to promote visibility and ensure that everyone's contributions are recognised and valued?

How can you, as an individual, prioritise your well-being while working remotely? What steps can you take to maintain a healthy work-life balance, manage stress, and prevent burnout?

As a leader, how can you model healthy behaviours, prioritise self-care, and create a culture that supports the well-being of your remote or hybrid team?

Reflect on the five key principles discussed in the chapter: connectivity, belonging, communication, visibility, and well-being support. Which of these principles do you believe your team currently excels in, and which areas provide the greatest opportunity for improvement?

Action

Implement a virtual open-door policy, such as setting aside dedicated time slots when your virtual door is open, and employees can drop in for informal conversations and check-ins.

Establish clear communication channels and protocols for your remote or hybrid team, ensuring everyone knows how and when to communicate using the appropriate tools and platforms.

Create regular opportunities for informal social interactions, such as virtual coffee breaks, casual check-ins, or online gaming sessions, to help team members connect on a personal level and build genuine relationships.

Develop a shared team identity and purpose by clearly articulating your team's mission, values, and goals, and consistently reinforcing this shared identity through regular team meetings and discussions.

Implement a "belonging check-in" at the start of each virtual team meeting, where team members share one thing that made them feel connected to the team that week, fostering a culture of empathy and understanding.

Prioritise visibility by conducting regular one-on-one meetings with team members, using technology for collaboration and connection and publicly celebrating team members' successes and milestones.

Model healthy behaviours and prioritise your well-being as a leader, openly discussing your well-being practices and challenges, and creating a culture that values and supports employee well-being.

AND FINALLY...

And finally...

Throughout this book, I have shared numerous examples of working with my clients and the success of the principles I have laid out. However, it is fair to ask whether the principles I have discussed genuinely create team resilience. To address this question, I would like to share a specific case study that demonstrates the effectiveness of my approach.

Over six months, I had the privilege of coaching a team at the charity MyVision Oxfordshire. The primary objective was to cultivate and enhance the team's resilience. You may be curious about how we can assess whether a team has indeed become more resilient. While resilience is often more anecdotal than a precise measurement, there are key indicators that can shed light on the team's progress. One significant indicator is observing how the team approaches and navigates challenges and adversity compared to their previous way of working. A more resilient team will demonstrate improved problem-solving skills, adaptability, and a proactive mindset when faced with obstacles. They will exhibit a greater capacity to bounce back from setbacks and maintain a positive outlook even in difficult circumstances. Another important aspect to consider is the team's overall performance. A resilient team is likely to experience higher levels of productivity, efficiency, and effectiveness. However, it is crucial to ensure that this enhanced performance is not achieved at the expense of the team members' well-being. A truly resilient team strikes a balance between delivering results and prioritising the physical, mental, and emotional health of its individuals. By observing these indicators—the team's approach to challenges, their performance, and their overall well-being—we can gain valuable insights into the development of their resilience over time. It is a subjective view that relies on the team's perception of their growth and improvement.

To establish a baseline and measure the team's progress in building resilience, I developed a comprehensive team resilience assessment tool at the outset of my engagement. This psychometric test was grounded in the research and findings from my Master's thesis in Psychology, ensuring a scientifically robust approach to evaluating the team's current level of resilience. By administering this assessment at the beginning of the process, I gained valuable insights into the team's strengths and areas for improvement, setting the stage for targeted interventions and strategies to enhance their collective resilience. Each team member answered 49 questions, which created a score across several components, including team learning, team flexibility, trust, and seven other areas. The initial assessment revealed that the team scored 69% overall on alignment, with alignment essentially measuring how closely the team members' views on resilience aligned with each other. Scores above 70% were considered strengths, while scores below 70% indicated areas that required further development.

For six months, I had the privilege of guiding the team through the transformative principles outlined in this book. By employing a holistic approach that combined facilitation, coaching and education, I aimed to equip the team with the tools and mindset necessary to cultivate resilience in the face of challenges. The engagement began with a focus on purpose—the foundation upon which resilient teams are built. Through interactive workshops and thought-provoking discussions, we explored the team's core values, mission, and vision. By articulating and aligning around a shared purpose, the team developed a stronger sense of unity and direction, laying the groundwork for the journey ahead. As we progressed, we turned our attention to developing and increasing psychological safety within the team. Recognising the importance of creating an environment where individuals feel comfortable taking risks, expressing vulnerabilities, and learning from failures, we implemented strategies to create trust, empathy, and open communication. Through exercises and candid conversations, the team gradually built a culture of psychological safety, enabling them to collaborate more effectively and navigate challenges with greater resilience.

Alongside the focus on purpose and psychological safety, we

also worked on building resilient processes. By examining existing workflows, identifying bottlenecks, and brainstorming solutions, the team developed a more agile and adaptable approach to their work. We introduced techniques such as scenario planning, regular debriefing sessions, and continuous improvement cycles, empowering the team to anticipate and respond to change with greater ease. Throughout the engagement, I also shared personal stories and insights on resilience, drawing from my own experiences as well as those of other leaders and teams. These narratives served as powerful examples, illustrating the practical application of resilience principles in real-world contexts. By relating to these stories, the team gained a deeper understanding of what it means to be resilient and how they could embody those qualities in their work.

It is worth noting that the entire engagement was conducted remotely, with sessions facilitated via Microsoft Teams. While the virtual format presented its own set of challenges, it also highlighted the importance of adaptability and resilience in the face of changing circumstances. Despite the physical distance, the team remained connected, engaged, and committed to their growth and development. As the six-month journey came to a close, the transformation within the team was evident. They had evolved into a more cohesive, confident, and resilient team, equipped with the tools and mindset to tackle any challenge that lay ahead. The combination of purpose, psychological safety, resilient processes, and personal resilience had forged a team that was not only prepared to weather storms but also to thrive when faced with adversity.

After completing the six-month programme, the team took the assessment again, and their overall alignment score increased to 71%. Although this may seem like a marginal gain, it represented a significant improvement in several individual components. For example, the trust component increased from 58% to 67%, and the team now had seven strengths (over 70%) compared to their initial five strengths. In addition to the quantitative results, the CEO provided valuable feedback on the impact of my work with their team. He stated, "Julian helped our team open up and have honest and constructive conversations. Over the past few months, Julian has brought out in us a desire to learn, grow, and challenge each other, to look at situations differently and to build stronger unity. I can highly recommend Julian, who expertly coached and facilitated our discussions around team resilience. Our charity is much better off, now having a stronger and deeper team relationship, ultimately improving our work and effectiveness. If you're unsure about investing the time and money - go for it, you will get it back tenfold!"

This case study demonstrates the tangible benefits of applying the principles and approaches I have shared throughout this book. By focusing on key components such as team learning, flexibility, and trust, teams can develop greater resilience and improve their ability to navigate challenges and adversity. The combination of quantitative data from the team resilience psychometric and qualitative feedback from Mark Upton, the CEO, provides compelling evidence that investing time and resources into building team resilience can yield significant returns. It is important to remember that making a team more resilient is an ongoing process that needs constant work and dedication. While the six-month programme with this charity team produced notable improvements, teams must maintain and build upon these gains by consistently applying the principles and strategies discussed in this book.

In conclusion, this case study serves as a testament to the effectiveness of the approach I have outlined for creating resilient teams. By focusing on key components, creating open communication, and providing expert guidance, teams can develop the skills and mindset necessary to thrive in the face of challenges and adversity. The positive outcomes achieved by this charity team underscore the value of investing in team resilience and the transformative impact it can have on an organisation's success and well-being.

As we conclude this exploration of team resilience, it's important to reflect on the key themes and takeaways that have emerged throughout the book. We've explored various facets of team resilience, from laying a solid foundation and cultivating individual and team strengths, to developing resilient leadership and embracing adaptability amidst change. However, the success of resilient teams is underpinned by two important elements: effective communication and a focus on well-being. These aspects serve as the glue that binds team members together. Recognising the pivotal role of communication and well-being in building resilient teams, I would like to share some further insights on the importance of communication and encourage you to read the chapter on remote and hybrid teams again regarding the well-being of your team. By prioritising these elements and integrating them into your team's daily operations, you can create a more supportive, collaborative, and resilient environment that empowers your team to reach new heights of success.

Communication

Effective communication is built on the foundation of empathy and understanding, which make it possible for leaders to develop more profound connections with the teams they are responsible for. As a leader of a team, you can build a culture of compassion and support by acknowledging and validating the feelings of the members of the team. This helps the team members become more resilient when confronted with challenges. You should make it a point to actively listen to the people in your team, displaying empathy and providing support to address the issues and concerns that they have. It is possible to ensure that all members of the team remain on the same page about the overarching aims and objectives by establishing regular communication. This can be accomplished through the use of emails, updates, or team huddles. Ensure you are both personable and accessible, embracing queries and providing answers as required to preserve trust and openness in your organisations.

When it comes to developing your communication messages, you should personalise your approach so that it resonates with the specific requirements and preferences of each member of your team. Leaders should have a good understanding of the distinct communication styles and preferences of each member of the team, to convey information effectively. Effective communication, feedback and reflection are essential components that enable you to continuously modify and enhance your approach. By soliciting input from members of the team regarding the effectiveness of communication and by reflecting on previous experiences with communication, you are able to identify areas in which you can make improvements. You may improve your ability to help your teams on their journey towards resilience and success by adopting a mentality that emphasises continual learning and growth. This allows them to continue to evolve their own communication tactics.

It is incredibly important to be clear and specific when communicating with your team, suppliers, or any audience, since lack of clarity can lead to misunderstandings, missed deadlines, and unsatisfactory results.

I have devised an acronym of **CLEAR** to help you communicate more effectively:

C - Clarity and being crystal clear: Take time to consider your audience, message, and the best format for communication. Use simple, concise language and tailor your message to your audience's background and perspective.

L - Listen actively: Fully concentrate on and comprehend the message being conveyed. Use nonverbal cues to show engagement and adjust your language based on the speaker's preferences and communication style.

E - Engage your audience: Understand your audience's needs, interests, and motivations. Use storytelling, examples, and analogies to make your points relatable and memorable. Appeal to their values and beliefs to engage them emotionally.

A - Ask questions: Use open-ended questions to gauge your audience's comprehension and encourage reflection and dialogue. Demonstrate that you value their input and perspectives to build trust and rapport.

R - Review your communication: Assess your audience's reception and identify areas where clarification may be needed. Restate key points, use examples or analogies to clarify complex ideas, and encourage questions. Review written communication for clarity, grammar, and tone.

To sum all of this up, I am fond of this quote by Oliver Wendell Holmes, Former Associate Justice of the Massachusetts Supreme Judicial Court (1841-1935), emphasising the importance of speaking clearly and thoughtfully: "Speak clearly, if you speak at all; carve every word before you let it fall."

Putting It All Together

Building resilient teams requires a holistic approach that encompasses all the elements explored throughout this book. By establishing a strong foundation, nurturing individual and team strengths, developing resilient leadership, embracing adaptability, prioritising effective communication, and focusing on well-being, teams can cultivate the resilience needed to navigate the challenges and opportunities of today's complex world. As you embark on your journey of building resilient teams, remember that the process is ongoing and iterative. It requires a commitment to continuous learning, experimentation, and growth. By staying curious, adaptable, and focused on the well-being of your team, you can create a culture of resilience that enables your team to thrive in the face of any challenge. By prioritising effective communication, focusing on well-being, and embracing the principles of resilience explored throughout this book, you and your team can navigate the challenges and opportunities ahead with confidence, adaptability, and strength. Together, you can build a culture of resilience that enables your team to thrive, no matter what the future may hold.

Icarus

A friend recently shared with me a part of the Icarus and Daedalus myth that I had never heard before, and it resonated with me as I was writing this book on building resilient teams. Most people are familiar with the part of the story where Icarus flies too close to the sun, causing his wings to melt and leading to his tragic downfall. However, there is another crucial aspect of the story that is often overlooked: Daedalus' warning to Icarus to not fly too low, near the sea, as the feathers could become saturated and lose their buoyancy.

As I conclude this book on building resilient teams, the myth of Icarus and Daedalus is a fitting analogy. Throughout the chapters, we have explored various strategies, techniques, and mindsets that contribute to team resilience. We have discussed the importance of embracing diversity, fostering psychological safety, creating resilient processes, and cultivating a sense of shared purpose. These elements are akin to the moderate flight path between the sun and the sea, as described in the myth. Just as Daedalus warned Icarus not to fly too close to the sun, leaders must be mindful of the risks of pushing their teams too hard. In the pursuit of ambitious goals and high performance, it is essential to recognise the potential for burnout and the importance of maintaining a sustainable pace. Teams that are constantly operating at their limits, without sufficient rest and support, are more likely to experience exhaustion, decreased morale, and ultimately, a breakdown in resilience. On the other hand, the myth's warning about flying too low, near the sea, reminds us of the dangers of complacency and inaction. Teams that become too comfortable, avoiding challenges and failing to push themselves, risk stagnation and a loss of resilience. Just as the feathers in the myth could become saturated and lose their buoyancy, teams that do not actively engage in growth, learning, and adaptation may find themselves ill-equipped to handle the ever-changing demands of their environment.

The key to building resilient teams lies in finding the right balance—a balance between pushing boundaries and maintaining sustainability, embracing challenges and providing support, and driving performance and prioritising well-being. As a leader, it is your responsibility to guide your team along this path, ensuring that they have the appropriate resources, skills, and mindset. Throughout this book, we have explored various strategies and approaches to help you achieve this balance. By creating a culture of psychological safety, you make it possible for team members to take risks, share their ideas, and learn from their mistakes. By embracing diversity and inclusivity, you tap into a wealth of perspectives and experiences that enhance problem-solving and innovation. By establishing a sense of shared purpose and meaning, you unite your team around a common goal and provide a foundation for resilience in the face of challenges. As you embark on the journey of building a resilient team, remember the lessons of Icarus and Daedalus. Seek the moderate path, the one that allows your team to soar while avoiding the pitfalls of burnout and complacency. Encourage open communication, provide support and resources, and create an environment that values balance, growth, and well-being. By doing so, you will not only build a team that can withstand the challenges of today but also one that is poised to thrive in the face of an uncertain future. Just as Daedalus' wings carried him to safety, your leadership and commitment to resilience will enable your team to navigate the ever-changing landscape of business and emerge stronger, more adaptable, and more successful than ever before.

Working with Julian

Are you ready to build a more resilient team that can thrive in any environment? As the author of "Weathering the Storm: A Guide to Building Resilient Teams," I offer personalised coaching and consultation services to help you implement the strategies and principles outlined in this book.

» What I offer

One-on-One Executive Coaching: Tailored sessions to develop your leadership skills and enhance your ability to build and lead resilient teams.

Team Resilience Workshops: Interactive sessions designed to assess your team's current resilience and develop strategies for improvement.

Customised Resilience-Building Programmes: Long-term engagements to transform your team or organisation's culture and practices.

» My approach

I believe in a collaborative, evidence-based approach that combines the latest research with practical, real-world strategies. My methods are adaptable to your unique context and challenges, ensuring that you get solutions that work for your specific situation.

» What you can expect

Deep insights into team dynamics and organisational behaviour.

Practical tools and techniques for building resilience.

Ongoing support and accountability.

Measurable improvements in team performance and adaptability.

» Ready to weather any storm?

Contact me at julian@julianrobertsconsulting.com to discuss how we can work together to build your team's resilience and set you up for long-term success.

Remember, resilience isn't just about surviving - it's about thriving in the face of adversity. Let's embark on this journey together.

Helping Organisations Thrive Podcast

Throughout this book, there are references to insights and interviews from my podcast, "Helping Organisations Thrive." This podcast serves as a complementary resource to the ideas and strategies presented in "Weathering the Storm," offering deeper dives into specific topics and real-world examples of resilient leadership in action.

» About the Podcast

"Helping Organisations Thrive" is a weekly podcast dedicated to exploring the cutting-edge ideas and practices that enable organisations to flourish in today's dynamic business environment. Each episode features in-depth conversations with thought leaders, Olympians, world record holders, successful executives, and experts in various fields related to organisational resilience and growth.

» What You'll Find

Interviews with resilient leaders sharing their experiences and lessons learned.

Discussions on emerging trends in organisational psychology and team dynamics.

Practical strategies for building more adaptable and innovative teams.

Insights into cultivating a culture of resilience and continuous improvement.

Expert advice on navigating change and uncertainty in the business world.

» Why Listen

The podcast serves as an ongoing resource for leaders and teams looking to stay at the forefront of organisational resilience. It's an excellent way to continue your learning journey beyond this book, hearing fresh perspectives and staying updated on the latest thinking in the field.

» Connect with the Podcast

Website: https://www.julianrobertsconsulting.com/podcast-1

The podcast is available on all major podcast platforms including Apple and Spotify.

I encourage you to tune in and join our community of leaders committed to building thriving, resilient organisations. Together, we can weather any storm and emerge stronger on the other side.

REFERENCES

Austin, R. D., & Pisano, G. P. (2017). Neurodiversity as a competitive advantage. Harvard Business Review, 95(3), 96-103.

Avolio, B.J. and Gardner, W.L. (2005). Authentic leadership development: Getting to the root of positive forms of leadership. *The Leadership Quarterly*, Volume 16, Issue 3, 2005, Pages 315-338.

Bandura, A. (1962). Social learning through imitation. In M.R. Jones (Ed), *Nebraska symposium on motivation*. 211-269. Nebraska Press.

Bandura, A. (1997). *Self Efficacy: The Exercise of Control*. Freeman, New York, NY.

Bass, B.M. and Steidlmeier, P. (1999). Ethics, character, and authentic transformational leadership behavior. *Leadership Quarterly*, 10(2), 181.

Bennett, J.B. , Aden, C.A. , Broome, K. , Mitchell, K. and Rigdon, W.D. (2010). "Team resilience for young restaurant workers: research-to-practice adaptation and assessment". *Journal of Occupational Health Psychology*, Vol. 15 No. 3, 223-236.

Blatt, R. (2009). "Resilience in entrepreneurial teams: developing the capacity to pull through".*Frontiers of Entrepreneurship Research*, Vol. 29 No. 11, 1-14.

Cameron, K. S., Dutton, J. E. and Quinn, R. E. (Eds.). (2003). *Positive organizational scholarship* (p. 55–74). San Francisco: Barrett-Kohler.

Deloitte. (2022). The connected worker: Driving resilience in the age of remote work.

Dixon-Fyle, S., Dolan, K., Hunt, V. and Prince, S. (2020). Diversity wins: How inclusion matters. McKinsey & Company. https://www.mckinsey.com/featured-insights/diversity-and-inclusion/diversity-wins-how-inclusion-matters

Duval, S. and Wicklund, R. A. (1972). *A theory of objective self-awareness*. Academic Press.

Duval, T. S. and Silvia, P. J. (2001). *Self-awareness and causal attribution: A dual-systems theory.* Boston: Kluwer Academic.

Duhigg, C. (2016). What Google learned from its quest to build the perfect team. The New York Times Magazine. https://www.nytimes.com/2016/02/28/magazine/what-google-learned-from-its-quest-to-build-the-perfect-team.html

Edmondson, A. C. (2018). The fearless organization: Creating psychological safety in the workplace for learning, innovation, and growth. John Wiley & Sons.

Ellis, D.G. and Fisher, B.A. (1994). *Small group decision-making: communication and the groupprocess* (4th ed.). New York: McGraw-Hill.

Emmons, R. A. and McCullough, M. E. (2003). Counting blessings versus burdens: An experimental investigation of gratitude and subjective well-being in daily life. *Journal of Personality and Social Psychology*, 84(2), 377-389.

Erickson, R. J. (1995). The importance of authenticity for self and society. *Symbolic Interaction*, 18(2),121–144.

Gardner, W.L. and Schermerhorn, J.R. (2004). Unleashing Individual Potential: Performance Gains Through Positive Organizational Behavior and Authentic Leadership. *Organizational Dynamics*, 33(3), 270-281.

Gardner, W.L., Avolio, B.J., Luthans, F., May, D.R. and

Walumbwa, F.O. (2005). Can you see the real me? A self-based model of authentic leader and follower development. *The Leadership Quarterly*, 16:343–72.

Gartner. (2022). Remote work trends: Navigating the challenges of virtual collaboration. Gierveld, J., Dykstra, P. A., and Schenk, N. (2012). Living arrangements, intergenerational support types and older adult loneliness in Eastern and Western Europe. *International Journal of Social Psychiatry*.

Glassdoor. (2020). Diversity & inclusion workplace survey: https://www.glassdoor.com/blog/glassdoors-diversity-and-inclusion-workplace-survey/

Groopman, J. (2004). *The Anatomy of Hope*. New York: Random House.

Harter, S. (2002). Authenticity. In C. R. Snyder, & S. Lopez (Eds.), *Handbook of positive psychology* (p.382–394). Oxford, UK: Oxford University Press.

Henderson, R., and Van den Steen, E. (2015). "Why Do Firms Have "Purpose"? The Firm's Role as a Carrier of Identity and Reputation." American Economic Review, 105 (5): 326-30.

Hewlett, S. A., Marshall, M. and Sherbin, L. (2013). How diversity can drive innovation. Harvard Business Review. https://hbr.org/2013/12/how-diversity-can-drive-innovation

Iqbal, N. and Ahmad Dar, K.A. (2018). The effect of social support, gratitude, resilience and satisfaction with life on depressive symptoms among police officers following Hurricane Katrina. *International Journal of Social Psychiatry*.

Kernis, M.H. (2003). Toward a conceptualization of optimal self-esteem. *Psychological Inquiry*, 14:1-26.

Korb, A. (2012). The Grateful Brain. *Psychology Today*.

Retrieved from https://www.psychologytoday.com/us/blog/prefrontal-nudity/201211/the-grateful-brain

Kozlowski, S.W.J. and Klein, K.J. (2000). A multilevel approach to theory and research inorganizations: Contextual, temporal, and emergent processes. In K.J. Klein & S.W.J.Kozlowski (Eds.), *Multilevel theory, research, and methods in organizations: Foundations, extensions, and new directions* (pp. 3–90). Jossey-Bass.

Lengnick-Hall, C.A., Beck, T.E. and Lengnick-Hall, M.L. (2011). Developing a capacity fororganizational resilience through strategic human resource management. *Human ResourceManagement Review*, 21(3), 243-255.

Lorenzo, R., Voigt, N., Tsusaka, M., Krentz, M. and Abouzahr, K. (2018). How diverse leadership teams boost innovation. Boston Consulting Group. https://www.bcg.com/publications/2018/how-diverse-leadership-teams-boost-innovation

Luthans, F. (2002). The need for and meaning of positive organizational behavior. *Journal ofOrganizational Behavior*, 23: 695-706.

Luthans, F. and Avolio, B. (2003), "Authentic leadership development", in Cameron, K.S. , Dutton, J.E.and Quinn, R.E. (Eds), *Positive Organisational Scholarship: Foundations of a New Discipline*, Berrett-Koehler, San Francisco, CA, 241-258.

Mathieu, J.E., Tannenbaum, S.I., Donsbach, J.S. and Alliger, G.M. (2014). A review and Integration of team composition models moving toward a dynamic and temporal framework. *Journal of Management*, 40(1), 130–160.

McKinsey & Company. (2022). The future of remote work: Adapting to the new normal.Microsoft. (2021).

Autism Hiring Program. Retrieved from https://www.microsoft.com/en-us/diversity/inside-microsoft/cross-disability/autismhiring.aspx

Microsoft. (2022). Work trend index: The hybrid work paradox.

Morgan, P.B.C, Fletcher, D. and Sarkar, M. (2013). *Defining and characterizing team resilience in elite sport*. Loughborough University. Journal contribution.

Nakamura, H., Tawatsuji, Y., Fang, S. and Matsui, T. (2021). Explanation of emotion regulation mechanism of mindfulness using a brain function model. *Neural Networks*, 138, 198-214.

Oracle. (2022). Mental health and remote work: Addressing the well-being imperative

PwC. (2022). Remote work survey: Visibility, recognition, and the new normal.

Roberts, J. (2022). Authentic leadership promotes team resilience. MSc Psychology thesis. Northumbria University.

Rousseau, V., Aubé, C. and Tremblay, S. (2013). Team coaching and innovation in work teams: An examination of the motivational and behavioral intervening mechanisms". *Leadership & Organization Development Journal*, 34, 344–364.

Seligman, M.E.P. (2002). *Authentic happiness: Using the new positive psychology to realize your potential for lasting fulfillment*. New York: Free Press.

Serra-Garcia, M., van Damme, E. and Potters, J. (2011). Hiding an inconvenient truth: Lies and vagueness. *Games and Economic Behavior*, 73(1), 244–261

Sisodia, R., Wolfe, D., and Sheth, J. (2007). Firms of

endearment: How world-class companies profit from passion and purpose.

Srámek P, Simecková M, Janský L, Savlíková J and Vybíral S. (2000) Human physiological responses to immersion into water of different temperatures. *Eur J Appl Physiol.* 81(5):436-42.

Sundstrom, E., De Meuse, K. P. and Futrell, D. (1990). Work teams: Applications and effectiveness. *American Psychologist*, 45(2), 120–133.

Sutcliffe, K. M. and Vogus, T. J. (2003). Organizing for resilience. *Positive organizational scholarship: Foundations of a new discipline*, 94, 110.

Tannenbaum, S. I. and Cerasoli, C. P. (2013). Do team and individual debriefs enhance performance? A meta-analysis. Human Factors, 55, 231–245.

Traylor, A.M., Tannenbaum, S.I., Thomas, E.J. and Salas, E. (2021). Helping healthcare teams save lives during COVID-19: Insights and countermeasures from team science. *American Psychologist*, Jan;76(1):1-13.

Tugade, M.M. and Fredrickson, B.L. (2004). Resilient individuals use positive emotions to bounce back from negative emotional experiences. *Journal of Personality and Social Psychology*, 86(2), 320–333.

Youssef, C.M. and Luthans, F. (2007). Positive organizational behavior in the workplace: The Impact of hope, optimism, and resilience. *Journal of Management*, 33(5), 774–800.

Walumbwa, F.O., Avolio, B.J., Gardner, W.L., Wernsing, T.S. and Peterson, S.J. (2008). Authentic leadership: Development and validation of a theory-based measure. *Journal of Management*, 34(1):89-126.

Printed in Great Britain
by Amazon